SELECTED POEMS 1923-1975

Random House New York

Robert Penn Warren

SELECTED POEMS

1923-1975

"Loss, of Perhaps Love, in Our World of Contingency," "Trying to Tell You Something," and "Old Nigger on One-Mule Cart Encountered Late at Night When Driving Home from Party in the Back Country" first appeared in *The New Yorker*. "A Way to Love God" and "Season Opens on Wild Boar in Chianti" were originally published in *The London Times*. "Evening Hawk" and "Midnight Outcry" originally appeared in *The Atlantic Monthly*. "Answer to Prayer" was first published in *The Virginia Quarterly*. "Brotherhood in Pain" first appeared in *The American Review*. "Paradox" was first published in *The New York Review of Books*.

Library of Congress Cataloging in Publication Data
Warren, Robert Penn, 1905–
    Selected poems, 1923–1975.
PS3545.A748A17 1976   811'.5'2   75–40551
ISBN 0–394–40531–5

A limited edition of this book has been privately printed.
Manufactured in the United States of America

9 8 7 6 5 4 3 2

First Trade Edition

Contents

AUDUBON

from TALE OF TIME *Poems 1960-1966*

xii

xiii

CAN I SEE ARCTURUS FROM WHERE I STAND?

Poems 1975

Is was *but a word for wisdom, its price?*
"RATTLESNAKE COUNTRY"

A WAY TO LOVE GOD

Here is the shadow of truth, for only the shadow is true.
And the line where the incoming swell from the sunset Pacific
First leans and staggers to break will tell all you need to know
About submarine geography, and your father's death rattle
Provides all biographical data required for the *Who's Who* of the dead.

I cannot recall what I started to tell you, but at least
I can say how night-long I have lain under stars and
Heard mountains moan in their sleep. By daylight,
They remember nothing, and go about their lawful occasions
Of not going anywhere except in slow disintegration. At night
They remember, however, that there is something they cannot remember,
So moan. Theirs is the perfected pain of conscience, that
Of forgetting the crime, and I hope you have not suffered it. I have.

I do not recall what had burdened my tongue, but urge you
To think on the slug's white belly, how sick-slick and soft,
On the hairiness of stars, silver, silver, while the silence
Blows like wind by, and on the sea's virgin bosom unveiled
To give suck to the wavering serpent of the moon; and,
In the distance, in *plaza, piazza, place, platz*, and square,
Boot heels, like history being born, on cobbles bang.

Everything seems an echo of something else.

And when, by the hair, the headsman held up the head
Of Mary of Scots, the lips kept on moving,
But without sound. The lips,
They were trying to say something very important.

But I had forgotten to mention an upland
Of wind-tortured stone white in darkness, and tall, but when
No wind, mist gathers, and once on the Sarré at midnight,
I watched the sheep huddling. Their eyes
Stared into nothingness. In that mist-diffused light their eyes
Were stupid and round like the eyes of fat fish in muddy water,
Or of a scholar who has lost faith in his calling.

*

Their jaws did not move. Shreds
Of dry grass, gray in gray mist-light, hung
From the side of a jaw, unmoving.

You would think that nothing would ever again happen.

That is a way to love God.

EVENING HAWK

From plane of light to plane, wings dipping through
Geometries and orchids that the sunset builds,
Out of the peak's black angularity of shadow, riding
The last tumultuous avalanche of
Light above pines and the guttural gorge,
The hawk comes.

        His wing
Scythes down another day, his motion
Is that of the honed steel-edge, we hear
The crashless fall of stalks of Time.

The head of each stalk is heavy with the gold of our error.

Look! look! he is climbing the last light
Who knows neither Time nor error, and under
Whose eye, unforgiving, the world, unforgiven, swings
Into shadow.

        Long now,
The last thrush is still, the last bat
Now cruises in his sharp heiroglyphics. His wisdom
Is ancient, too, and immense. The star
Is steady, like Plato, over the mountain.
    *

If there were no wind we might, we think, hear
The earth grind on its axis, or history
Drip in darkness like a leaking pipe in the cellar.

LOSS, OF PERHAPS LOVE,
IN OUR WORLD OF CONTINGENCY

Think! Think hard. Try to remember
When last you had it. There's always

A logic to everything, and you are a part
Of everything, and your heart bleeds far

Beyond the outermost pulsar. Put your mind on
The problem, and under no circumstances look

In the mirror, for you might not
Recognize what you see there, and the night wind

Shuffles a torn newspaper down the street with a sound
Like an old bum's old shoe-soles that he makes

Slide on the pavement to keep them from flopping off.
Shut your eyes, think hard, it doesn't really

Matter which end you start from—forward from
The earliest thing you remember, the dapple

Of sunlight on the bathroom floor while your mother
Bathed you, or backward from just now when

You found it gone and cried out, *oh Jesus, no!* Yes,
Forward or backward, it's all the same,
          *

To the time you are sure you last had it. Violets,
Buried now under dead leaves (later snowdrifts), dream

How each, with a new-born, dew-bright eye, will see
You again pass, cleaving the blue air.

Oh, bestiaries!—

Myths, and moraines where the basalt boulders, moonlit, grieve
And the dark little corner under your bed, where God

Huddles tight in the fluff-ball, like a cocoon, that He,
All-knowing, knows the vacuum won't find!

Think hard. Take a deep breath. As the thunder-clap
Dissolves into silence, your nostrils thrill to the

Stunned new electric tang of joy—or pain—like ammonia.

We must learn to live in the world.

ANSWER TO PRAYER
A Short Story That Could Be Longer

In that bad year, in a city to have now no name,
In the already-dark of a winter's day, our feet
Unsteady in slip-tilt and crunch of re-freezing snow as if lame,
And two hands ungloved to clasp closer though cold, down a side street

We moved. Ahead, intersecting, stretched the avenue where
Life clanged and flared like a gaudy disaster under
Whatever the high sky wombed in its dark imperative of air,
And where, to meat and drink set, we might soon pretend, or
        *

At least hope, that sincerity could be bought by pain.
But now stopped. She said, "Wait!" And abrupt, was gone
Up the snow-smeared broad stone to dark doors before I could restrain
That sentimental idiocy. Alone,

As often before in a night-street, I raised eyes
To pierce what membrane remotely enclosed the great bubble of light
                                                                that now
The city inflated against the dark hover of infinities,
And saw how a first frail wavering stipple of shadow

Emerged high in that spectral concavity of light, and drew down to be,
In the end, only snow. Then she, again there, to my question, replied
That she had made a prayer. And I: "For what?" And she:
"Nothing much, just for you to be happy." Then cocking her head to one
                                                                side,

Looked up and grinned at me, an impudent eye-sparkling grin, as though
She had just pulled the trick of the week, and on a cold-flushed
Cheek, at the edge of the grin for an accent, the single snow-
Flake settled, and gaily in insult she stuck her tongue out, and blood rushed

To my heart. So with hands again nakedly clasped, through the soft veil
                                                                and swish
Of flakes falling, we moved toward the avenue. And later, proceeded,
Beyond swirl and chain-clank of traffic, and a siren's far anguish,
To the unlit room to enact what comfort body and heart needed.

Who does not know the savvy insanity and wit
Of history! and how its most savage peripeteia always
Has the shape of a joke—if you find the heart to laugh at it.
In such a world, then, one must be pretty careful how one prays.

Her prayer, yes, was answered, for in spite of my meager desert,
Of a sudden, life—it was bingo! was bells and all ringing like mad,
Lights flashing, fruit spinning, the machine spurting dollars like dirt—
Nevada dollars, that is—but all just a metaphor for the luck I now had.

But that was long later, and as answer to prayer long out
Of phase. And now thinking of her, I can know neither what, nor where,

She may be, and even in gratitude, I must doubt
That she ever remembers she ever prayed such a prayer.

Or if she remembers, she laughs into the emptiness of air.

PARADOX

Running ahead beside the sea,
You turned and flung a smile, like spray.
It glittered like tossed spray in the sunlight.
Yes, well I remember, to this day,
That glittering ambiguity.

I saw, when your foot fulfilled its stride,
How the sand, compressed, burst to silver light,
But when I had reached that aureoled spot
There was only another in further flight:
And bright hair, wind-strung, to tease the sun's pride.

Yes, far away and long ago,
In another land, on another shore,
That race you won—even as it was lost,
For if I caught you, one moment more,
You had fled my grasp, up and to go

With glowing pace and the smile that mocks
Pursuit down whatever shore reflects
Our flickering passage through the years,
As we enact our more complex
Version of Zeno's paradox.

MIDNIGHT OUTCRY

Torn from the dream-life, torn from the life-dream,
Beside him in darkness, the cry bursts: *Oh!*
Endearment and protest—they avail
Nothing against whatever is so
Much deeper and darker than anything love may redeem.

He lies in the dark and tries to remember
How godlike to strive in passion and sweat,
But fears to awaken and clasp her, lest
Their whole life be lost, for he cannot forget
That the depths that cry rose from might shrivel a heart, or member.

How bright dawns morning!—how sweetly the face
Inclines over the infant to whom she gives suck.
So his heart leaps in joy, but remembering
That echo of fate beyond faith or luck,
He fixes his studious gaze on the scene to trace

In the least drop spilled between nipple and the ferocious
Little lip-suction, some logic, some white
Spore of the human condition that carries,
In whiteness, the dark need that only at night
Finds voice—but only and always one strange to us.

The day wore on, and he would ponder,
Lifting eyes from his work, thinking, thinking,
Of the terrible distance in love, and the pain,
Smiling back at the sunlit smile, even while shrinking
From recall of the nocturnal timbre, and the dark wonder.

TRYING TO TELL YOU SOMETHING

To Tinkum Brooks

All things lean at you, and some are
Trying to tell you something, though of some

The heart is too full for speech. On a hill, the oak,
Immense, older than Jamestown or God, splitting

With its own weight at the great inverted
Crotch, air-spread and ice-hung, ringed with iron

Like barrel-hoops, only heavier, massive rods
Running through and bolted, and higher, the cables,

Which in summer are hidden by green leaves—the oak,
It is trying to tell you something. It wants,

In its fullness of years, to describe to you
What happens on a December night when

It stands alone in a world of snowy whiteness. The moon is full.
You can hear the stars crackle in their high brightness.

It is ten below zero, and the iron
Of hoops and reinforcement rods is continuing to contract.

There is the rhythm of a slow throb, like pain. The wind,
Northwest, is steady, and in the wind, the cables,

In a thin-honed and disinfectant purity, like
A dentist's drill, sing. They sing

Of truth, and its beauty. The oak
Wants to declare this to you, so that you

Will not be unprepared when, some December night,
You stand on a hill, in a world of whiteness, and

    *

Stare into the crackling absoluteness of the sky. The oak
Wants to tell you because, at that moment,

In your own head, the cables will sing
With a thin-honed and disinfectant purity,

And no one can predict the consequences.

BROTHERHOOD IN PAIN

Fix your eyes on any chance object. For instance,
That leaf, prematurely crimson, of the swamp maple

That dawdles down gold air to the velvet-black water
Of the moribund beaver-pond. Or the hunk

Of dead chewing gum in the gutter with the mark of a molar
Yet distinct on it, like the most delicate Hellenistic chisel-work.

Or a black sock you took off last night and by mistake
Left lying, to be found in the morning, on the bathroom tiles.

Or pick up a single stone from the brookside, inspect it
Most carefully, then throw it back in. You will never

See it again. By the next spring flood, it may have been hurled
A mile downstream. Fix your gaze on any of these objects,

Or if you think me disingenuous in my suggestions,
Whirl around three times like a child, or a dervish, with eyes shut,

Then fix on the first thing seen when they open.
In any case, you will suddenly observe an object in the obscene moment
                                                    of birth.

        *

It does not know its own name. The matrix from which it is torn
Bleeds profusely. It has not yet begun to breathe. Its experience

Is too terrible to recount. Only when it has completely forgotten
Everything, will it smile shyly, and try to love you,

For somehow it knows that you are lonely, too.
It pityingly knows that you are more lonely than it is, for

You exist only in the delirious illusion of language.

SEASON OPENS ON WILD BOAR IN CHIANTI
To Guerino and Ginevra Roberti

They are hunting the boar in the vineyards.
They halloo and hunt in the pine-glen.
Their voices in distance are music.
Now hounds have the scent, they make music.
The world is all music, we listen:
Men are hunting because they are mere men.

Gold light of October falls over
The vineyards and dark bulbs exposed there.
The blood of the great boar has thickened
With grapes, and oak-mast on the ridges.
He is full of years, and now waits where
His tusks gleam white in the dark air.

Since sunrise the halloo and music
Has filled all the vineyards, and wild ground.
Music echoed among the high pine boughs.
It was heard where the oak leaf cast shadow.
Now where rushes are trampled, is no sound.
Dead too, at the tusk-point, the best hound.
        *

In the twilight and silence, now passing
Our door, men pant with the heavi-
ness of their destiny's burden,
Each wondering who will be able
To choose his own ground when the adversary
Encounters him, red eye to red eye.

The boar stood well backed by the river,
His flanks safe in a cavern of rushes.
In front was only the whole world.
But who cares for that, it is simple—
The moiling of dogs and scared dashes,
Men's halloo and stupid fire-flashes?

The delicate, razor-sharp feet, not
Now dancing, now dancing, point starward.
They are lashed to a pole swung from shoulders
So the great head swings weighty and thoughtful
While eyes blank in wisdom stare hard
At the foot-gravel grinding slow forward.

Thus onward they pass in the nightfall,
The great head swinging down, tusks star-gleaming.
The constellations are steady.
The wind sets in from the northeast.
And we bolt up our doors, thus redeeming,
From darkness, our ignorant dreaming.

OLD NIGGER ON ONE-MULE CART ENCOUNTERED LATE AT NIGHT WHEN DRIVING HOME FROM PARTY IN THE BACK COUNTRY

Flesh, of a sudden, gone nameless in music, flesh
Of the dancer, under your hand, flowing to music, girl-
Flesh sliding, flesh flowing, sweeter than

Honey, slicker than Essolube, over
The music-swayed, delicate trellis of bone
That is white in secret flesh-darkness. What
The music, it says: *no name, no name!*—only
That movement under your hand, what
It is, and no name, and you shut your eyes, but
The music, it stops. O.K. Silence
Rages, it ranges the world, it will
Devour us, for
That sound I do now hear is not external, is
Simply the crinkle and crepitation,
Like crickets gone nuts, of
Booze in the blood. *Goodnight! Goodnight!*

I can't now even remember the name of the dancer, but

I must try to tell you what, in July, in Louisiana,
Night is. No moon, but stars whitely outrageous in
Blackness of velvet, the long lane ahead
Whiter than snow, wheels soundless in deep dust, dust
Pluming whitely behind, and ahead all
The laneside hedges and weed-growth
Long since powdered whiter than star-dust, or frost, but air
Hot. The night pants hot like a dog, it breathes
Off the blossoming bayou like the expensive whiff
Of floral tributes at a gangster's funeral in N.O.,
It breathes the smell love makes in darkness, and far off,
In the great swamp, an owl cries,
And does not stop. At the sharp right turn,
Hedge-blind, which you take too fast,
There it is: death-trap.

On the fool-nigger, ass-hole wrong side of
The road, naturally: And the mule-head
Thrusts at us, and ablaze in our headlights,
Outstaring from primal bone-blankness and the arrogant
Stupidity of skull snatched there
From darkness and the saurian stew of pre-Time,
For an instant—the eyes. The eyes,
They blaze from the incandescent magma

Of mule-brain. Thus mule-eyes. Then
Man-eyes, not blazing, white-bulging
In black face, in black night, and man-mouth
Wide open, the shape of an O, for the scream
That does not come. Even now,
That much in my imagination, I see. But also
The cargo of junk the black face blooms amidst—
Rusted bed-springs on end, auto axle at God-knows-what
Angle up-canted, barbed wire on a fence rail wound,
Lengths of stove pipe beat up. God-yes,
A death-trap. But
I snatch the wheel left in a dust-skid,
Smack into the ditch, but the ditch
Shallow, and so, not missing a beat, I'm out
And go on, and he's left alone on his cart there
Unmoving, and dust of the car's passage settles
White on sweat-sticky skin, black, of the forehead, and on
The already gray head. This,
Of course, under the high stars.

Perhaps he had screamed, after all.

And go on: to the one last drink, sweat-grapple in darkness, then
Sleep. But only until
The hour when small, though disturbing, gastric shifts
Are experienced, the hour when the downy
Throat of the swamp owl vibrates to the last
Predawn cry, the hour
When joy-sweat, or night-sweat, has dried to a microscopic
Crust on the skin, and some
Recollection of childhood brings tears
To dark-wide eyes, and the super-ego
Again throws the switch for the old recorded harangue.
Until waking, that is—and I wake to see
Floating in darkness above the bed the
Black face, eyes white-bulging, mouth shaped like an O, and so
Get up, get paper and pencil, and whittle away at
The poem. Give up. Back to bed. And remember
Now only the couplet of what
Had aimed to be—Jesus Christ—a sonnet:

One of those who gather junk and wire to use
For purposes that we cannot peruse.

As I said, Jesus Christ. But

Moved on through the years. Am here. Another
Land, another love, and in such latitude, having risen
In darkness, feet bare to cold boards, stare,
Through ice-glitter of glass and air purer
Than absolute zero, into
The white night and star-crackling sky over
The snow-mountain. Have you ever,
At night stared into the snow-filled forest and felt
The impulse to flee there? Enter there? Be
There and plunge naked
Through snow, through drifts floundering, white
Into whiteness, among
Spectral great beech-boles, birch-whiteness, black jag
Of shadow, black spruce-bulks snow-shouldered, floundering
Upward and toward the glacial assertion that
The mountain is? Have you ever
Had the impulse to stretch forth your hand over
The bulge of forest and seize trees like the hair
Of a head you would master? Well,
We are entitled to our fantasies, for life
Is only the fantasy that has happened to us, and

In God's name. But

In the lyrical logic and nightmare astuteness that
Is God's name, by what magnet, I demand,
Are the iron and out-flung filings of our lives, on
A sheet of paper, blind-blank as Time, snapped
Into a polarized pattern—and I see,
By a bare field that yearns pale in starlight, the askew
Shack. He arrives there. Unhitches the mule.
Stakes it out. Between cart and shack,
Pauses to make water, and while
The soft, plopping sound in deep dust continues, his face
Is lifted into starlight, calm as prayer. He enters

The dark shack, and I see
A match spurt, then burn down, die.

The last glow is reflected on the petal-pink
And dark horn-crust of the thumbnail.

And so I say:
Brother, Rebuker, my Philosopher past all
Casuistry, will you be with me when
I arrive and leave my own cart of junk
Unfended from the storm of starlight and
The howl, like wind, of the world's monstrous blessedness,
To enter, by a bare field, a shack unlit?
Entering into that darkness to fumble
My way to a place to lie down, but holding,
I trust, in my hand, a name—
Like a shell, a dry flower, a worn stone, a toy—merely
A hard-won something that may, while Time
Backward unblooms out of time toward peace, utter
Its small, sober, and inestimable
Glow, trophy of truth.

Can I see Arcturus from where I stand?

from

OR ELSE—
Poem/Poems 1968-1974

To Cesare and Rysia Lombroso

He clave the rocks in the wilderness and gave them drink as out of the great depths.
                              —PSALMS: 78:15

I
THE NATURE OF A MIRROR

The sky has murder in the eye, and I
Have murder in the heart, for I
Am only human.
We look at each other, the sky and I.
We understand each other, for

The solstice of summer has sagged, I stand
And wait. Virtue is rewarded, that
Is the nightmare, and I must tell you

That soon now, even before
The change from Daylight Saving Time, the sun,
Beyond the western ridge of black-burnt pine stubs like
A snaggery of rotten shark teeth, sinks
Lower, larger, more blank, and redder than
A mother's rage, as though
F.D.R. had never run for office even, or the first vagina
Had not had the texture of dream. Time

Is the mirror into which you stare.

INTERJECTION # 1:
THE NEED FOR RE-EVALUATION

Is this really me? Of course not, for Time
Is only a mirror in the fun-house.

You must re-evaluate the whole question.

II
NATURAL HISTORY

In the rain the naked old father is dancing, he will get wet.
The rain is sparse, but he cannot dodge all the drops.

He is singing a song, but the language is strange to me.

The mother is counting her money like mad, in the sunshine.
Like shuttles her fingers fly, and the sum is clearly astronomical.

Her breath is sweet as bruised violets, and her smile sways like
                                        daffodils reflected in a brook.

The song of the father tells how at last he understands.
That is why the language is strange to me.

That is why clocks all over the continent have stopped.

The money the naked old mother counts is her golden memories of love.
That is why I see nothing in her maniacally busy fingers.

That is why all flights have been canceled out of Kennedy.

As much as I hate to, I must summon the police.
For their own good, as well as that of society, they
                                        must be put under surveillance.

They must learn to stay in their graves. That is what graves are for.

III
TIME AS HYPNOSIS
For I. A. Richards

White, white in that dawnlight, the world was exploding, white
Light bursting from whiteness. What
Is the name of the world?—for

Whiteness, all night from the black sky unfeathering,
Had changed the world's name, and maybe
My own, or maybe it was all only
A dream I was having, but did not
Know it, or maybe the truth was that I,
Huddling tight in the blankets and darkness and self,
Was nothing, was nothing but what
The snow dreamed all night. Then light:

Two years and no snow in our section, and two years
Is a long time when you are twelve. So,

All day in a landscape that had been
Brown fields and black woods but was now
White emptiness and arches,
I wandered. The white light
Filled all the vertiginous sky, and even
My head until it
Spread bright and wide like another sky under which I
Wandered. I came
To a place where the woods were, stood under
A crazed geometry of boughs black but
Snow-laden and criss-crossed with light, and between
Banks of humped snow and whiteness of ice-fret, saw
Black water slide slow, and glossy as sleep.

I stared at the water, and staring, wondered
What the white-bellied minnow, now deep in
Black leaf-muck and mud, thought.
I thought of the muskrat dim in his mud-gloom.
    *

Have you ever seen how delicately
Etched the print of the field mouse's foot in fresh snow is?
I saw the tracks. But suddenly, none. Nothing
But the wing-flurried snow. Then, small as a pin-head, the single
Bright-frozen, red bead of a blood-drop. Have you ever
Stared into the owl's eyes? They blink slow, then burn:
Burn gold in the dark inner core of the snow-shrouded cedar.

There was a great field that tilted
Its whiteness up to the line where the slant, blue knife-edge of sky
Cut it off. I stood
In the middle of that space. I looked back, saw
My own tracks march at me. Mercilessly,
They came at me and did not stop. Ahead,
Was the blankness of white. Up it rose. Then the sky.

Evening came, and I sat by the fire, and the flame danced.

All day, I had wandered in the glittering metaphor
For which I could find no referent.

All night, that night, asleep, I would wander, lost in a dream
That was only what the snow dreamed.

IV
BLOW, WEST WIND

I know, I know—though the evidence
Is lost, and the last who might speak are dead.
Blow, west wind, blow, and the evidence, O,

Is lost, and wind shakes the cedar, and O,
I know how the kestrel hung over Wyoming,
Breast reddened in sunset, and O, the cedar
*

Shakes, and I know how cold
Was the sweat on my father's mouth, dead.
Blow, west wind, blow, shake the cedar, I know

How once I, a boy, crouching at creekside,
Watched, in the sunlight, a handful of water
Drip, drip, from my hand. The drops—they were bright!

But you believe nothing, with the evidence lost.

INTERJECTION # 2:
CAVEAT

For John Crowe Ransom

Necessarily, we must think of the
world as continuous, for if it were
not so I would have told you, for I have
bled for this knowledge, and every man
is a sort of Jesus, but in any
case, if it were not so, you wouldn't know
you are in the world, or even that the
world exists at all—

                    but only, oh, on-
ly, in discontinuity, do we
know that we exist, or that, in the deep-
est sense, the existence of anything
signifies more than the fact that it is
continuous with the world.

                    A new high-
way is under construction. Crushed rock has
been spread for miles and rolled down. On Sunday,
when no one is there, go and stand on the
roadbed. It stretches before your eyes in-

to distance. But fix your eyes firmly on
one fragment of crushed rock. Now, it only
glows a little, inconspicuously
one might say. But soon, you will notice a
slight glittering. Then a marked vibration
sets in. You brush your hand across your eyes,
but, suddenly, the earth underfoot is
twitching. Then, remarkably, the bright sun
jerks like a spastic, and all things seem to
be spinning away from the univer-
sal center that the single fragment of
crushed rock has ineluctably become.

At this point, while there is still time and will,
I advise you to detach your gaze from
that fragment of rock. Not all witnesses
of the phenomenon survive unchanged
the moment when, at last, the object screams

in an ecstasy of

being.

V
I AM DREAMING OF A WHITE CHRISTMAS:
THE NATURAL HISTORY OF A VISION
For Andrew Vincent Corry

[1]
No, not that door—never! But,
Entering, saw. Through
Air brown as an old daguerreotype fading. Through
Air that, though dust to the tongue, yet—
Like the inward, brown-glimmering twilight of water—

Swayed. Through brown air, dust-dry, saw. Saw
It.

    The bed.

          Where it had
Been. Now was. Of all
Covering stripped, the mattress
Bare but for old newspapers spread.
Curled edges. Yellow. On yellow paper dust,
The dust yellow. No! Do not.

                  Do not lean to
Look at that date. Do not touch
That silken and yellow perfection of Time that
Dust is, for
There is no Time. I,
Entering, see.

       I,
Standing here, breathe the dry air.

    [2]
              See
Yonder the old Morris chair bought soon
After marriage, for him to rest after work in, the leather,
Once black, now browning, brown at the dry cracks, streaked
With a fungoid green. Approaching,
See.

    See it.

      The big head. Propped,
Erect on the chair's leather pillow, bald skin
Tight on skull, not white now, brown
Like old leather lacquered, the big nose
Brown-lacquered, bold-jutting yet but with
Nostril-flanges gone tattered in Time. I have not

Yet looked at the eyes. Not
Yet.

     The eyes
Are not there. But,
Not there, they stare at what
Is not there.

    [3]
         Not there, but
In each of the appropriate twin apertures, which are
Deep and dark as a thumb-gouge,
Something that might be taken for
A mulberry, large and black-ripe when, long back, crushed,
But now, with years, dust-dried. The mulberries,
Crushed and desiccated, each out of
Its dark lurking-place, stare out at
Nothing.

       His eyes
Had been blue.

    [4]
         Hers brown. But
Are not now. Now staring,
She sits in the accustomed rocker, but with
No motion. I cannot
Be sure what color the dress once was, but
Am sure that the fabric now falls decisively away
From the Time-sharpened angle of knees. The fabric
Over one knee, the left, has given way. And
I see what protrudes.

        See it.

         Above,
The dry fabric droops over breastlessness.
    *

Over the shrouded femurs that now are the lap, the hands,
Palm-down, lie. The nail of one forefinger
Is missing.

On the ring-finger of the left hand
There are two diamond rings. On that of the right,
One. On Sundays, and some evenings
When she sat with him, the diamonds would be on the fingers.

The rings. They shone.

Shine now.

In the brown air.

On the brown-lacquered face
There are now no
Lips to kiss with.

[5]
The eyes had been brown. But
Now are not where eyes had been. What things
Now are where eyes had been but
Now are not, stare. At the place where now
Is not what once they
Had stared at.

There is no fire on the cold hearth now,
To stare at.

[6]
        On
The ashes, gray, a piece of torn orange peel.
Foil wrappings of chocolates, silver and crimson and gold,
Yet gleaming from grayness. Torn Christmas paper,
Stamped green and red, holly and berries, not
Yet entirely consumed, but warped
And black-gnawed at edges. I feel

Nothing. A red
Ribbon, ripped long ago from some package of joy,
Winds over the gray hearth like
A fuse that failed. I feel
Nothing.

        Not even
When I see the tree.

Why had I not seen the tree before?
Why, on entering, had I not seen it?
It must have been there, and for
A long time, for
The boughs are, of all green, long since denuded.
That much is clear. For the floor
Is there carpeted thick with the brown detritus of cedar.

Christmas trees in our section always were cedar.

[7]
Beneath the un-greened and brown-spiked tree,
On the dead-fall of brown frond-needles, are,
I see, three packages. Identical in size and shape.
In bright Christmas paper. Each with red bow, and under
The ribbon, a sprig of holly.

        But look!

           The holly
Is, clearly, fresh.

I say to myself:

       The holly is fresh.

          And
My breath comes short. For I am wondering
Which package is mine.
    *

Oh, which?

I have stepped across the hearth and my hand stretches out.

But the voice:

No presents, son, till the little ones come.

[8]
What shadow of tongue, years back unfleshed, in what
Darkness locked in a rigid jaw, can lift and flex?

The man and the woman sit rigid. What had been
Eyes stare at the cold hearth, but I
Stare at the three chairs. Why—
Tell me why—had I not observed them before? For
They are here.

              The little red chair,
For the baby. The next biggest chair
For my little sister, the little red rocker. Then,
The biggest, my own, me the eldest.

The chairs are all empty.

                    But
I am thinking a thought that is louder than words.
Thinking:

       They're empty, they're empty, but me—oh, I'm here!

And that thought is not words, but a roar like wind, or
The roar of the night-freight beating the rails of the trestle,
And you under the trestle, and the roar
Is nothing but darkness alive. Suddenly,
Silence.

        And no
Breath comes.

[9]
                    Where I was,
Am not. Now am
Where the blunt crowd thrusts, nudges, jerks, jostles,
And the eye is inimical. Then,
Of a sudden, know:

                         Times Square, the season
Late summer and the hour sunset, with fumes
In throat and smog-glitter at sky-height, where
A jet, silver and ectoplasmic, spooks through
The sustaining light, which
Is yellow as acid. Sweat,
Cold in arm-pit, slides down flesh.

The flesh is mine.

What year it is, I can't, for the life of me,
Guess, but know that,
Far off, south-eastward, in Bellevue,
In a bare room with windows barred, a woman,
Supine on an iron cot, legs spread, each ankle
Shackled to the cot-frame,
Screams.

She keeps on screaming because it is sunset.

Her hair has been hacked short.

    [10]
Clerks now go home, night watchmen wake up, and the heart
Of the taxi-driver, just coming on shift,
Leaps with hope.

All is not in vain.

Old men come out from the hard-core movies.
They wish they had waited till later.
        *

They stand on the pavement and stare up at the sky.
Their drawers are drying stiff at the crotch, and
The sky dies wide. The sky
Is far above the first hysteria of neon.

Soon they will want to go and get something to eat.

Meanwhile, down the big sluice of Broadway,
The steel logs jerk and plunge
Until caught in the rip, snarl, and eddy here before my face.

A mounted policeman sits a bay gelding. The rump
Of the animal gleams expensively. The policeman
Is some sort of dago. His jowls are swart.
His eyes are bright with seeing.

He is as beautiful as a law of chemistry.

[11]
In any case,
I stand here and think of snow falling. But am
Not here. Am
Otherwhere, for already,
This early and summer not over, in West Montana—
Or is it Idaho?—in
The Nez Percé Pass, tonight
It will be snowing.

The Nez Percé is more than 7,000 feet, and I
Have been there. The first flakes,
Large, soft, sparse, come straight down
And with enormous deliberation, white
Out of unbreathing blackness. Snow
Does not yet cling, but the tall stalk of bear-grass
Is pale in darkness. I have seen, long ago,
The paleness of bear-grass in darkness.

                              But tell me, tell me,
Will I never know

What present there was in that package for me,
Under the Christmas tree?

[12]
All items listed above belong in the world
In which all things are continuous,
And are parts of the original dream which
I am now trying to discover the logic of. This
Is the process whereby pain of the past in its pastness
May be converted into the future tense

Of joy.

INTERJECTION # 3:
I KNOW A PLACE WHERE ALL IS REAL
For Austin Warren

I know a place where all is real. I
have been there, therefore
know. Access is not easy, the way
rough, and visibility extremely poor, especially
among the mountains. Maps
show only the blank space, somewhere
northwest of Mania and beyond Delight,
but if you can manage to elude the natives of
intervening zones, who practice
ghastly rites and have an appetite for human flesh,
you may find a sly track through
narrow and fog-laced passes. Meanwhile
give little credence to tales told
by returning travelers or those
who pretend to be such. But truth,
sometimes, is even more unacceptable
to the casual hearer, and in bars

I have been laughed at for reporting
the simple facts.

                    In any case,
few travelers do return.
Among those who choose to remain and apply
for naturalization, a certain number
find that they cannot stand the altitude, but these,
upon making their way out, sometimes die of an oppressive
pulmonary complaint as soon as they hit the low country.

VI
BALLAD OF MISTER DUTCHER
AND THE LAST LYNCHING IN GUPTON

He must have been just as old in
days when young as later, his face
as gray and his eyes not gray but
that color there's not even a
name for—all this the same as when,
years later, he'd walk down the street,
and I, a boy, would then see him
in his worn-out gray coat going
twice a day to the depot, where
he'd handle what express came, then
twice a day going back home, the
first time to eat, the last to shut
the door of his small gray house, and
not be seen till tomorrow, and
if ever you said hello, he
might say whatever it was that
you never quite caught, but always
his face had a sort of gray smile
turned more inside than out, as though

there was something he knew but knew
that you'd never know what it was he knew.

He had a small wife whose face was
as gray as the gingham she wore,
or the gray coat that on Sunday
she wore to church, and nobody
could ever imagine what, in
that small gray house, those gray faces
might ever say to each other,
or think, as they lay side by side
while his eyes of that color you
couldn't ever name stared up where
dark hid the ceiling. But we knew
how he'd smile in the dark who knew
that he knew what we'd never know he knew.

But time brings all things to light, so
long after the gray-faced wife was
dead, and the hump of her grave sunk
down to a trench, and the one gray-
faced son dead to boot, having died
one cold winter night in jail, where
the town constable had put him
to sober up—well, long after,
being left all alone with his
knowledge of what we'd never know he knew,

he, in the fullness of time, and
in glory, brought it forth. One hot
afternoon in Hoptown, some fool
nigger, wall-eyed drunk and with a
four-bit hand-gun, tried to stick up
a liquor store, shot the clerk, and,
still broke, grabbed a freight, and was high-
tailing for Gupton, in happy
ignorance that the telephone
had ever been invented. So
when they flagged down the freight, the fool
nigger made one more mistake, up

and drilled one of the posse. That
was that, and in five minutes he
was on his way to the county
seat, the constable driving, but
mighty slow, while back there
in Gupton, in the hardware store,
a business transaction concern-
ing rope was in due process. It
was the small gray-faced man who, to
general astonishment though
in a low, gray voice, said: "Gimme
that rope." Quick as a wink, six turns
around the leader, the end snubbed,
and there was that neat cylinder
of rope the noose line could slide through
easy as a greased piston or
the dose of salts through the widow-
woman, and that was what Mister
Dutcher, all the days, weeks, and years,
had known, and nobody'd known that he knew.

The constable, it sort of seemed,
had car trouble, and there he was
by the road, in the cooling shade
of a big white oak, with his head
stuck under the hood and a wrench
in his hand. They grabbed him before
he even got his head out, which,
you could tell, was not in any
great hurry anyway. Well, what
happened was not Mister Dutcher's
fault, nor the rope's, it was only
that that fool nigger just would not
cooperate, for when the big
bread truck they had him standing on
drew out, he hung on with both feet
as long as possible, then just
keeled over, slow and head-down, in-
to the rope, spilling his yell out
like five gallons of fresh water

in one big, bright, out-busting slosh
in the sunshine, if you, of a
sudden, heave over the crock. So,
that fool nigger managed never
to get a good, clean drop, which was,
you might say, his last mistake. One
man started vomiting, but one
put six .44's in, and that
quieted down the main performer.
Well, that was how we came to know
what we'd all thought we'd never know he knew.

But isn't a man entitled
to something he can call truly
his own—even to his pride in
that one talent kept, against the
advice of Jesus, wrapped in a
napkin, and death to hide? Any-
way, what does it matter now, for
Mister Dutcher is not there to
walk the same old round like a blind
mule hitched to a sorghum mill, is,
in fact, in some nook, niche, crack or
cubby of eternity, stowed
snug as a bug, and safe from all
contumely, wrath, hurt ego, and
biologic despair, with no
drop of his blood to persist in
that howling orthodoxy of
darkness that, like speed-hurled rain on
glass, streams past us, and is Time. At
all events, I'm the one man left
who has any reason at all
to remember his name, and if
truth be told, I haven't got so
damned much, but some time, going back,
I might try to locate the stone
it's on, if grass and ragweed aren't too high.
                    *

I might even try to locate
where that black man got buried, though
that would, of course, be somewhat difficult.

VII
CHAIN SAW AT DAWN IN VERMONT
IN TIME OF DROUTH

1.

Dawn and, distant, the steel-snarl and lyric
Of the chain saw in deep woods:
I wake. Was it
Trunk-scream, bough-rip and swish, then earth-thud?
No—only the saw's song, the saw
Sings: *now!* Sings:
Now, now, now, in the
Lash and blood-lust of an eternal present, the present
Murders the past, the nerve shrieks, the saw

Sings *now,* and I wake, rising
From that darkness of sleep which
Is the past, and is
The self. It is
Myself, and I know how,
Now far off,
New light gilds the spruce-tops.
The saw, for a moment, ceases, and under
Arm-pits of the blue-shirted sawyer sweat
Beads cold, and
In the obscene silence of the saw's cessation,
A crow, somewhere, calls.
           *

The crow, in distance, calls with the crystalline beauty
Of the outraged heart.

Have I learned how to live?

2.

On the other side of the woods, in the village, a man
Is dying. Wakes
In dawn to the saw's song, thinks
How his wife was a good wife, wonders
Why his boy turned out bad, wonders why
He himself never managed to pay off the mortgage, thinks
Of dawn and the first light spangling the spruces, and how
He leaned on the saw and the saw
Sang. But had not known what
The saw sang. So now thinks:
I have not learned how to die, but

For that thought has no language, has only
The saw's song, in distance: glee of steel and the
Sun-shriek, the scream of castration, the whirl-tooth hysteria
Of *now, now, now!* So
Sweats. What

Can I tell him? I
Cannot tell him how to die because
I have not learned how to live—what man
Has learned how to live?—and I lie

In the dawn, and the thin sheet of summer
Lies on me, and I close my eyes, for
The saw sings, and I know
That soon I must rise and go out in the world where
The heel of the sun's foot smites horridly the hill,
And the stalk of the beech leaf goes limp,
And the bright brook goes gray among boulders,
And the saw sings, for

*

I must endeavor to learn what
I must learn before I must learn
The other thing. If
I learn even a little, I may,
By evening, be able
To tell the man something.

Or he himself may have learned by then.

VIII
SMALL WHITE HOUSE

The sun of July beats down on the small white house.
The pasture is brown-bright as brass, and like brass, sings with heat.
Halt! And I stand here, hills shudder, withdraw into distance,
Leprous with light. And a child's cry comes from the house.

Tell me, oh, where, in what state, did I see the small white house,
Which I see in my mind?—And the wax-wing's beak slices the blue
                                        cedar-berry,
Which is as blue as distance. The river, far off, shrinks
Among the hot boulders, no glister, looks dead as a discarded snake-skin
                                        rubbed off on stone. The house

Swims in that dazzle of no-Time. The child's cry comes from the house.

INTERJECTION # 4:
BAD YEAR, BAD WAR:
A NEW YEAR'S CARD, 1969

And almost all things are by the law purged
with blood; and without shedding of blood
there is no remission.
                    Epistle to the Hebrews, 9:22.

That was the year of the bad war. The others—
Wars, that is—had been virtuous. If blood

Was shed, it was, in a way, sacramental, redeeming
Even evil enemies from whose veins it flowed,

Into the benign logic of History; and some,
By common report even the most brutalized, died with a shy

And grateful smile on the face, as though they,
At the last, understood. Our own wounds were, of course, precious.

There is always imprecision in human affairs, and war
Is not exception, therefore the innocent—

Though innocence is, it should be remembered, a complex concept—
Must sometimes suffer. There is the blunt

Justice of the falling beam, the paw-flick of
The unselective flame. But happily,

If one's conscience attests to ultimate innocence,
Then the brief suffering of others, whose innocence is only incidental,

Can be regarded, with pity to be sure, as merely
The historical cost of the process by which

The larger innocence fulfills itself in
The realm of contingency. For conscience

Is, of innocence, the final criterion, and the fact that now we
Are troubled, and candidly admit it, simply proves
        *

That in the past we, being then untroubled,
Were innocent. Dear God, we pray

To be restored to that purity of heart
That sanctifies the shedding of blood.

IX
FOREVER O'CLOCK

1.

A clock is getting ready to strike forever o'clock.
I do not know where the clock is, but it is somewhere.
I know it is somewhere, for I can hear it trying to make
  up its mind to strike.
Somewhere is the place where it is while it is trying to
  make up its mind.
The sound it makes trying to make up its mind is purely metaphysical.
The sound is one you hear in your bloodstream and not your ear.
You hear it the way a man tied to a post in the yard of the
  State Penitentiary of Utah
Could hear the mind of the Deputy Warden getting ready to
  say, "Fire!"
You hear it the way you hear your wife's breathing back in a dark room
  at home, when
You are away on a trip and wake up in some hotel bedroom, and do
  not know offhand where you are and do not know whose breath
  you do hear there beside you.

2.

The clock is taking time to make up its mind and that is why I
  have time
To think of some things that are not important but simply are.
A little two-year-old Negro girl-baby, with hair tied up in spindly
  little tits with strings of red rag,

43

Sits in the red-clay dust. Except for some kind of rag around her
middle, she is naked, and black as a ripe plum in sunshine.
Behind the child is a gray board shack, and from the mud-chimney
a twist of blue smoke is motionless against the blue sky.
The fields go on forever, and what had been planted there is not
there now. The drouth does not see fit to stop even now.
The pin-oak in the yard has been dead for years. The boughs are
black stubs against the blue sky.
Nothing alive is here but the child and a dominecker hen, flattened
puff-belly down, under the non-shade of the pin-oak.

Inside the gray feathers, the body of the hen pants with heat.
The yellow beak of the hen is open, and the flattened string-
thin tongue looks black and dry and sharp as a pin.
The naked child with plum-black skin is intensely occupied.
From a rusted tin snuff can in the right hand, the child pours
red dust over the spread fingers of the left hand held out
prone in the bright air.
The child stares at the slow-falling red dust. Some red dust piles
precariously up on the back of the little black fingers thrust
out. Some does not.
The sun blazes down on the naked child in the mathematical center
of the world. The sky glitters like brass.
A beat-up old 1931 Studebaker, of a kind you are too young ever
to have seen, has recently passed down the dirt road, and a
plume of red dust now trails it toward the horizon.
I watch the car that I know I am the man driving as it recedes
into distance and approaches the horizon.

3.

I have now put on record one thing that is not important but
simply is.
I watch the beat-up old green Studebaker moving like a dot into
distance trailing its red plume of dust toward the horizon.
I wonder if it will ever get there. The wondering throbs like a
bruise inside my head.
Perhaps it throbs because I do not want to know the answer to
my wondering.

The sun blazes down from the high center of the perfect concavity
of sky. The sky glitters like brass.

A clock somewhere is trying to make up its mind to strike forever
o'clock.

X
RATTLESNAKE COUNTRY

For James Dickey

1.
Arid that country and high, anger of sun on the mountains, but
One little patch of cool lawn:

                    Trucks
Had brought in rich loam. Stonework
Held it in place like a shelf, at one side backed
By the length of the house porch, at one end
By rock-fall. Above that, the mesquite, wolf-waiting. Its turn
Will, again, come.

                    Meanwhile, wicker chairs, all day,
Follow the shimmering shade of the lone cottonwood, the way that
Time, sadly seeking to know its own nature, follows
The shadow on a sun-dial. All day,
The sprinkler ejects its misty rainbow.

                    All day,
The sky shivers white with heat, the lake,
For its fifteen miles of distance, stretches
Tight under the white sky. It is stretched
Tight as a mystic drumhead. It glitters like neurosis.
You think it may scream, but nothing
Happens. Except that, bit by bit, the mountains
Get heavier all afternoon.
          *

One day,
When some secret, high drift of air comes eastward over the lake,
Ash, gray, sifts minutely down on
Our lunch-time ice cream. Which is vanilla, and white.

There is a forest fire on Mount Ti-Po-Ki, which
Is at the western end of the lake there.

2.

If, after lunch, at God's hottest hour,
You make love, flesh, in that sweat-drench,
Slides on flesh slicker than grease. To grip
Is difficult.

At drink-time,
The sun, over Ti-Po-Ki, sets
Lopsided, and redder than blood or bruised cinnabar, because of
The smoke there. Later,
If there is no moon, you can see the red eyes of fire
Wink at you from
The black mass of the mountain.

At night, in the dark room, not able to sleep, you
May think of the red eyes of fire that
Are winking from blackness. You may,
As I once did, rise up and go from the house. But,
When I got out, the moon had emerged from cloud, and I
Entered the lake. Swam miles out,
Toward the moonset. Motionless,
Awash, metaphysically undone in that silvered and
Unbreathing medium, and beyond
Prayer or desire, saw
The moon, slow, swag down, like an old woman's belly.

Going back to the house, I gave the now-dark lawn a wide berth.

At night the rattlers come out from the rock-fall.
They lie on the damp grass for coolness.

3.

I-yee!—

   and the wranglers, they cry on the mountain, and waking
At dawn-streak, I hear it.

            High on the mountain
I hear it, for snow-water there, snow long gone, yet seeps down
To green the raw edges and enclaves of forest
With a thin pasturage. The wranglers
Are driving our horses down, long before daylight, plunging
Through gloom of the pines, and in their joy
Cry out:

      I-yee!

         We ride this morning, and,
Now fumbling in shadow for *levis*, pulling my boots on, I hear
That thin cry of joy from the mountain, and what I have,
Literally, seen, I now in my mind see, as I
Will, years later, in my mind, see it—the horsemen
Plunge through the pine-gloom, leaping
The deadfall—*I-yee!*—
Leaping the boulder—*I-yee!*—and their faces
Flee flickering white through the shadow—*I-yee!*—
And before them,
Down the trail and in dimness, the riderless horses,
Like quicksilver spilled in dark glimmer and roil, go
Pouring downward.

         The wranglers cry out.

                  And nearer.

                        But,
Before I go for my quick coffee-scald and to the corral,
I hear, much nearer, not far from my open window, a croupy
Gargle of laughter.

         It is Laughing Boy.

4.

Laughing Boy is the name that my host—and friend—gives his yard-hand.
Laughing Boy is Indian, or half, and has a hare-lip.
Sometimes, before words come, he utters a sound like croupy laughter.
When he utters that sound his face twists. Hence the name.

Laughing Boy wakes up at dawn, for somebody
Has to make sure the rattlers are gone before
The nurse brings my host's twin baby daughters out to the lawn.
Laughing Boy, who does not like rattlers, keeps a tin can
Of gasoline covered with a saucer on an outer ledge of the porch.
Big kitchen matches are in the saucer. This
At the porch-end toward the rock-fall.

The idea is: Sneak soft-foot round the porch-end,
There between rattlers and rock-fall, and as one whips past,
Douse him. This with the left hand, and
At the same instant, with the nail of the right thumb,
Snap a match alight.

                     The flame,
If timing is good, should, just as he makes his rock-hole,
Hit him.

The flame makes a sudden, soft, gaspy sound at
The hole-mouth, then dances there. The flame
Is spectral in sunlight, but flickers blue at its raw edge.

Laughing Boy has beautiful coordination, and sometimes
He gets a rattler. You are sure if
The soft, gasping sound and pale flame come before
The stub-buttoned tail has disappeared.

                          Whenever
Laughing Boy really gets a rattler, he makes that sound like
Croupy laughter. His face twists.

Once I get one myself. I see, actually, the stub-buttoned tail
Whip through pale flame down into earth-darkness.
       *

"The son-of-a-bitch," I am yelling, "did you see me, I got him!"

I have gotten that stub-tailed son-of-a-bitch.

I look up at the sky. Already, that early, the sky shivers with whiteness.

5.

What was *is* is now *was*. But
Is *was* but a word for wisdom, its price? Some from
That long-lost summer are dead now, two of the girls then young,
Now after their pain and delusions, worthy endeavors and lies, are,
Long since, dead.

The third
Committed her first adultery the next year, her first lover
A creature odd for her choosing, he who
Liked poetry and had no ambition, and
She cried out in his arms, a new experience for her. But
There were the twins, and she had, of course,
Grown accustomed to money.

Her second,
A man of high social position, who kept a score-card. With her,
Not from passion this time, just snobbery. After that,
From boredom. Forgot, finally,
The whole business, took up horse-breeding, which
Filled her time and even, I heard, made unneeded money, and in
The old news photo I see her putting her mount to the jump.
Her yet beautiful figure is poised forward, bent elbows
Neat to her tight waist, face
Thrust into the cleansing wind of her passage, the face
Yet smooth as a girl's, no doubt from the scalpel
Of the plastic surgeon as well as
From her essential incapacity
For experience.
*

                The husband, my friend,
Would, by this time, be totally cynical. The children
Have been a disappointment. He would have heavy jowls.
Perhaps he is, by this time, dead.

As for Laughing Boy, he wound up in the pen. Twenty years.
This for murder. Indians
Just ought to leave whiskey to the white folks.

I can't remember the names of the others who came there,
The casual weekend-ers. But remember

What I remember, but do not
Know what it all means, unless the meaning inheres in
The compulsion to try to convert what now is *was*
Back into what was *is*.

                I remember
The need to enter the night-lake and swim out toward
The distant moonset. Remember
The blue-tattered flick of white flame at the rock-hole
In the instant before I lifted up
My eyes to the high sky that shivered in its hot whiteness.

And sometimes—usually at dawn—I remember the cry on the mountain.

All I can do is to offer my testimony.

XI
HOMAGE TO THEODORE DREISER
On the Centennial of His Birth (August 27, 1871)

Oh, the moon shines fair tonight along the Wabash,
From the fields there comes the breath of new mown hay.
Thro' the sycamores the candle lights are gleaming,
On the banks of the Wabash, far away.

The Refrain of "On the Banks of the Wabash, Far Away"
Words by Theodore Dreiser and Paul Dresser
Music by Paul Dresser

I. PSYCHOLOGICAL PROFILE

Who is the ugly one slump-slopping down the street?
Who is the chinless wonder with the potato-nose?
Can't you hear the soft *plop* of the pancake-shaped feet?

He floats, like Anchises' son, in the cloud of his fine new clothes,
Safe, safe at last, from the street's sneer, toward a queen who will fulfill
The fate devised him by Venus—but where, oh when! That
is what he never knows

Born with one hand in his pants and one in the till,
He knows that the filth of self, to be loved, must be clad in glory,
So once stole twenty-five dollars to buy a new coat, and that is why still

The left eye keeps squinting backward—yes, history
Is gum-shoeing closer behind, with the constable-hand that clutches.
Watch his mouth, how it moves without sound, he is telling
himself his own old story.

Full of screaming his soul is, and a stench like live flesh that scorches.
It's the screaming, and stench, of a horse-barn aflame,
And the great beasts rear and utter, their manes flare up like torches.

From lies, masturbation, vainglory, and shame,
He moves in his dream of ladies swan-necked, with asses ample and sweet,
But knows that no kiss heals his soul, it is always the same.

*

The same—but a brass band plays in the distance, and the midnight cricket,
Though thinly, asseverates his name. He seeks amid the day's traffic a
                                                                    sign—
Some horseshoe or hunchback or pin—that now, at last, at the end of
                                                            this street

He will enter upon his reality: but enters only in-
To your gut, or your head, or your heart, to enhouse there and stay,
And in that hot darkness lie lolling and swell—like a tumor, perhaps
                                                            benign.

May I present Mr. Dreiser? He will write a great novel, someday.

2. VITAL STATISTICS
   [A]
Past Terre Haute, the diesels pound,
Eastward, westward, and under the highway slab the ground,
Like jello, shakes. Deep
In the infatuate and foetal dark, beneath
The unspecifiable weight of the great
Mid-America loam-sheet, the impacted
Particular particles of loam, blind,
Minutely grind.

At that depth and with that weight,
The particles, however minutely, vibrate
At the incessant passage
Of the transcontinental truck freight,
And concerning that emperor whose gut was god, Tacitus
Wrote, "ex urbe atque Italia inritamenta gulae gestabantur . . . ,"
And from both
Adriatic and Tyrrhenian seas, sea-crayfish and bivalve and,
Glare-eyed, the mullet, redder than flame,
Surrendered themselves in delight
To soothe that soft gullet wheredown all honor and empire
Slid slick, and wheels all night
Hummed on the highways to guarantee prompt delivery.
          *

Saliva gathers in the hot darkness of mouth-tissue. The mouth,
Slack, drools at the corners, but ever so little.

                                        All night,
Past Terre Haute, tires, on the concrete, scream, and in that town,
Long before the age of the internal combustion engine, but not
Before that of gewgaw, gilt, and grab, when the war
For freedom had just given place to the war for the dollar,
Theodore Dreiser was born. That was on South Ninth Street, but
The exact address is, of course, lost. He was born
Into the vast anonymity of the poor.

                              Have you ever
Seen moonlight on the Wabash, far away?

   [B]
On the wrong side of the tracks—that was where
He was born, and he never let you forget it, and his sisters
Had hot crotches and round heels.
He knew the gnaw of hunger, and how the first wind of winter feels.
He was born into the age of conspicuous consumption, and knew
How the heart, in longing, numbly congeals.

Nothing could help nothing, not reading Veblen or even Freud, for
The world is a great ass propped high on pillows, the cunt
Winks.

      Dreiser,
However, could not feel himself worthy. Not,
At least, of love. His nails,
Most horribly, were bitten. At night,
Sometimes, he wept. The bed springs
Creaked with the shift of his body, which,
In the Age of Faith and of Contempt of the World,
Would have been called a sack
Of stercorry: i.e., that matter the body ejects.
      *

Sometimes he wept for the general human condition,
But he was hell on women.

He had never loved any woman, he confessed,
Except his mother, whose broken shoes, he,
In childhood, had once caressed,
In the discovery of pity.

                    Have you ever
Seen midnight moonlight on the Wabash,
While the diesel rigs boom by?
Have you ever thought how the moonlit continent
Would look from the tearless and unblinking distance of God's wide eye?

     3. MORAL ASSESSMENT
You need call no psychiatrist
To anatomize his pain.
He suffers but the pain all men
Suffer in their human kind.
No—suffers, too,
His nobility of mind.

He denies it, he sneers at it,
In his icy nightmare of
The superlative of self;
Tries to, but cannot theorize past
The knowledge that
Others suffer, too, at last.

He is no philosopher.
His only gift is to enact
All that his deepest self abhors,
And learn, in his self-contemptive distress,
The secret worth
Of all our human worthlessness.

XII
FLAUBERT IN EGYPT

For Dorothea Tanning

Winterlong, off La Manche, wind leaning. Gray stones of the gray
    city sluiced by gray rain. And he dreamed

Of desert and distance, sunlight like murder, lust and new colors whose
    names exploded the spectrum like dynamite,
    or cancer. So went there,

Who did not know what he was, or could be, though hoping he might
    find there his fate. Found
    what he found: with head shaven,

One lock at the occiput left, red tarboosh wind-flaunted, rode hard at
    the Sphinx, at the "Father of Terrors," which,
    in that perspective and distance, lifted slow from
    the desert, like a great ship from hull-down.
    At its height,
    it swung. His cry burst forth.

In the white-washed room, by the light of wicks in three oil-glasses and to
    the merciless *screak* of the rebec, with musicians
    blind-folded, the dancer, her breasts
    cruelly bound to bulge upward and bare, above
    pink trousers, flesh rippling in bronze, danced
    the dance which

He recalls from the oldest Greek vases—the leap on one foot with
    the free foot crossed over, the fingers
    aquiver, face calm, and
    slow centuries sifting like shadow. Light
    flickers on whitewash. He finds
    the *mons veneris* shaven, arse noble.
    That night three *coups*, and once
    performs cunnilingus. Fingers clutching her necklace,
    he lies. He remembers his boyhood. Her fingers
    and naked thighs twitch in sleep.
    *

By day, on the minaret-top, the stork clacked its beak. At the edge of
    the carrion-field, the wild dog,
    snout blue from old blood,
    skulked, and camel bells in the distance.
    On the voyage down-Nile, on the slave-boat, old women,
    black and slaves too, who had seen all of life, tried
    to persuade the young girls, market-bound,
    to smile. But once,

On the height of Gebel Abusir, looking down on the Cataract, where
    the Nile flung itself to white froth on black granite, he
    cried out: "Eureka—the name, it is Emma!"
    And added: "Bovary." Pronouncing the *o*,
    as recorded by his companion, quite short.

So home, and left Egypt, which was: palms black, sky red, and the river
    like molten steel, and the child's hand
    plucking his sleeve—"*Baksheesh*,
    and I'll get you my mother to fuck"—and the bath-boy
    he buggered, this in a clinical spirit and as
    a tribute to the host-country. And the chancre, of course,
    bright as a jewel on his member, and borne
    home like a trophy.

But not to be omitted: on the river at Thebes, having long stared
    at the indigo mountains of sunset, he let
    eyes fix on the motion of three wave-crests that,
    in unison, bowed beneath the wind, and his heart
    burst with a solemn thanksgiving to God for
    the fact he could perceive the worth of the
    world with such joy.

Years later, death near, he remembered the palm fronds—
    how black against a bright sky!

INTERJECTION # 5:
SOLIPSISM AND THEOLOGY

Wild with ego, wild with world-blame,
He stared at the up-heave and enormity of ocean.
He said: *It does not even know my name.*

Wild with ego, wild with grief,
He stared at the antic small aphid green on the green leaf.
He said: *It has a home, but I—I'm the lost one.*

Wild with ego, wild with despair,
He stared at the icy and paranoid glitter of winter stars.
He said: *They would grind me like grain, small as dust, and not care.*

Wild with ego, wild with weeping,
He stared at the classic shut eyelids of his true love sleeping.
He said: *She sleeps, and the wild boar gashes my groin.*

Wild with ego, wild with wrong,
He stared into the dark pit of self whence all had sprung.
He said: *What is man that I should be mindful of him!*

But was—he was—and even yearned after virtue.

XIII
THE TRUE NATURE OF TIME

I. THE FARING

Once over water, to you borne brightly,
Wind off the North Sea cold but
Heat-streaked with summer and honed by the dazzle
Of sun, and the Channel boat banging

57

The chop like a shire-horse on cobbles—thus I,
Riding the spume-flash, by gull cries ringed,
Came.

Came, and the harbor slid smooth like an oil-slick.
It was the gray city, but the gray roof-slates
Sang blue in the sun, and the sea-cliffs,
Eastward, swung in that blue wind. I came thus,
And I, unseen, saw. Saw
You,

And you, at the pier edge, face lifting seaward
And toward that abstract of distance that I
Yet was and felt myself to be, stood. Wind
Tugged your hair. It tangled that brightness. Over
Your breast wind tautened the blue cloth, your skirt
Whipped, your bare legs were brown. Steel
Rang on steel. Shouts
Rose in that language.
Later,

The quiet place. Roses. Yellow. We came there, wind
Down now, sea slopping the rocks, slow, sun low and
Sea graying, but roses were yellow, climbing
The wall, it was stone. The last light
Came gilding a track across the gray water from westward.
It came leveling in to finger the roses. One
Petal, yellow, fell, slow.

At the foot of the gray stone, like light, it lay.
High beyond roses, a gull, in the last light, hung.

The sea kept slopping the rocks, slow.

2. THE ENCLAVE

Out of the silence, the saying. Into
The silence, the said. Thus
Silence, in timelessness, gives forth
Time, and receives it again, and I lie
            *

In darkness and hear the wind off the sea heave.
Off the sea, it uncoils. Landward, it leans,
And at the first cock-crow, snatches that cry
From the cock's throat, the cry,
In the dark, like gold blood flung, is scattered. How

May I know the true nature of Time, if
Deep now in darkness that glittering enclave
I dream, hangs? It shines. Another
Wind blows there, the sea-cliffs,
Far in that blue wind, swing. Wind

Lifts the brightening of hair.

XIV
VISION UNDER THE OCTOBER MOUNTAIN:
A LOVE POEM

Golding from green, gorgeous the mountain
high hangs in gold air, how
can stone float, it is

the image of authority, of reality—or, is it?—floating
with no weight, and glows, did we
once in the womb dream, dream
a gold mountain in gold
air floating, we in the

pulse and warm slosh of
that unbreathing bouillon, lulled in
the sway of that sweet
syllogism—oh, unambiguous—swung
in the tide of that bliss unbreathed, bathed in
un-self which was self, did we
dream a gold mountain, did

it glow in that faceless unfatuous
dark, did
it glow in gold air in the airless
abstraction of dark, floating high
above our blind eyes with

no lashes yet, unbrined by grief yet, we
seeing nothing, but
what did we dream—a
gold mountain,
floating?

I want to understand the miracle
of your presence here by my side, your
gaze on the mountain. I want

to hear the whole story of how
you came here, with
particular emphasis on the development of

the human scheme of values.

XV
STARGAZING

The stars are only a backdrop for
The human condition, the stars
Are brilliant above the black spruces,
And fall comes on. Wind

Does not move in the star-stillness, wind
Is afraid of itself, as you have been afraid in
Those moments when destruction and revelation
Have spat at each other like cats, and the mirror
Showed no breath, ha, ha, and the wind,
*

Far off in arctic starlight, is afraid
To breathe, and waits, huddled in
Sparse blackness of spruces, black glitter in starlight, in
A land, north, where snow already is, and waits:

And the girl is saying, "You do not look
At the stars," for I did not look at
The stars, for I know they are there, know
That if I look at the stars, I

Will have to live over again all I have lived
In the years I looked at stars and
Cried out, "O reality!" The stars
Love me. I love them. I wish they

Loved God, too. I truly wish that.

INTERJECTION # 6:
WHAT YOU SOMETIMES FEEL ON
YOUR FACE AT NIGHT

Out of mist, God's
Blind hand gropes to find
Your face. The fingers
Want to memorize your face. The fingers
Will be wet with the tears of your eyes. God

Wants only to love you, perhaps.

XVI
LITTLE BOY AND LOST SHOE

The little boy lost his shoe in the field.
Home he hobbled, not caring, with a stick whipping goldenrod.
Go find that shoe—I mean it, right now!
And he went, not now singing, and the field was big.

Under the sky he walked and the sky was big.
Sunlight touched the goldenrod, and yellowed his hair,
But the sun was low now, and oh, he should know
He must hurry to find that shoe, or the sun will be down.

Oh, hurry, boy, for the grass will be tall as a tree.
Hurry, for the moon has bled, but not like a heart, in pity.
Hurry, for time is money and the sun is low.
Yes, damn it, hurry, for shoes cost money, you know.

I don't know why you dawdle and do not hurry.
The mountains are leaning their heads together to watch.
How dilatory can a boy be, I ask you?

                              Off in Wyoming,
The mountains lean. They watch. They know.

XVII
COMPOSITION IN GOLD AND RED-GOLD

Between the event and the word, golden
The sunlight falls, between
The brown brook's braiding and the mountain it
Falls, in pitiless plenitude, and every leaf
On the ruined apple tree is gold, and the apples all
Gold, too, especially those
    *

On the ground. The gold of apples
That have fallen flushes to flame, but
Gold is the flame. Gold
Goes red-gold—and the scene:

A chipmunk is under the apple tree, sits up
Among gold apples, is
Golden in gold light. The chipmunk
Wriggles its small black nose
In the still center of the world of light.

The hair of the little girl is as brown-gold as
Brook water braiding in sunlight.

The cat, crouching by the gray stone, is gold, too.
The tail of the cat, half-Persian, weaves from side to side,
In infinite luxury, gold plume
Of sea-weed in that tide of light.
That is a motion that puts
The world to sleep.

The eyes of the cat are gold, and

I want to sleep. But
The event: the tiny
Shriek unstitches the afternoon, the girl
Screams, the sky
Tingles crystalline like a struck wine glass, and you
Feel the salt thickening, like grit, in your secret blood. Afterward

There is a difference in the quality of silence.
Every leaf, gold, hangs motionless on the tree, but
There is a difference in the quality of
Motionlessness: unverbed, unverved, they
Hang. On the last day will the sun
Explode? Or simply get too tired?

The chipmunk lies gold among the apples.
It is prone and totally relaxed like ripe
Fruit fallen, and,

Upon closer inspection, you can see
The faint smear of flame-gold at the base
Of the skull. This effect
Completes the composition.

The little girl
Holds the cat in her arms,
Crooning, "Baby, oh, baby." She weeps under
The powerful flood of gold light.

Somewhere, in the shade of alders, a trout
Hangs steady, head against a current like ice.

The eagle I had earlier seen climbing
The light tall above the mountain is

Now beyond sight.

INTERJECTION # 7:
REMARKS OF SOUL TO BODY

(On the Occasion of a Birthday Party)
For Sergio and Alberta Perosa

You've toughed it out pretty well, old Body, done
Your duty, and gratified most of my whims, to boot—
Though sometimes, no doubt, against your better judgment,
Or even mine—and are still
Revving over satisfactorily, considering.

Keep doing your duty, yes, and some fine day
You'll get full pension, with your every need
Taken care of, and not a dime out of your own pocket—
Or anybody's pocket, for that matter—for you won't have
Any needs, not with the rent paid up in perpetuity.
    *

But now tonight, to recognize your faithful service,
We've asked a few friends in, with their Bodies, of course—
Many of those Bodies quite charming, in fact—and after
You've drunk and dined, then you and all the other Bodies
Can go for a starlit romp, with the dogs, in the back pasture.

And we, the Owners—of Bodies, not dogs, I mean—
We'll sit by the fire and talk things over, remark
The baroque ironies of Time, exchange
Some childhood anecdotes, then on to the usual topics,
The death of the novel, the plight of democracy, and naturally, Vietnam.

But let us note, too, how glory, like gasoline spilled
On the cement in a garage, may flare, of a sudden, up,

In a blinding blaze, from the filth of the world's floor.

XVIII
THERE'S A GRANDFATHER'S CLOCK IN THE HALL

There's a grandfather's clock in the hall, watch it closely. The
    minute hand stands still, then it jumps, and in between jumps
    there is no-Time,
And you are a child again watching the reflection of early morning
    sunlight on the ceiling above your bed,

Or perhaps you are fifteen feet under water and holding your breath
    as you struggle with a rock-snagged anchor, or holding your
    breath just long enough for one more long, slow thrust to make
    the orgasm really intolerable,
Or you are wondering why you really do not give a damn, as they
    trundle you off to the operating room,
    *

Or your mother is standing up to get married and is very pretty,
      and excited and is a virgin, and your heart overflows, and
      you watch her with tears in your eyes, or
She is the one in the hospital room and she is really dying.

They have taken out her false teeth, which are now in a tumbler
      on the bedside table, and you know that only the undertaker
      will ever put them back in.
You stand there and wonder if you will ever have to wear false
      teeth.

She is lying on her back, and God, is she ugly, and
With gum-flabby lips and each word a special problem, she is
      asking if it is a new suit that you are wearing.

You say yes, and hate her uremic guts, for she has no right to make
      you hurt the way that question hurts.
You do not know why that question makes your heart hurt like a
      kick in the scrotum,

For you do not yet know that the question, in its murderous triviality,
      is the last thing she will ever say to you,
Nor know what baptism is occurring in a sod-roofed hut or hole on
      the night-swept steppes of Asia, and a million mouths, like
      ruined stars in darkness, make a rejoicing that howls like
      wind, or wolves,

Nor do you know the truth, which is: *Seize the nettle of innocence
      in both your hands, for this is the only way, and every*
*Ulcer in love's lazaret may, like a dawn-stung gem, sing—or even
      burst into whoops of, perhaps, holiness.*

But, in any case, watch the clock closely. Hold your breath
      and wait.
Nothing happens, nothing happens, then suddenly, quick as a
      wink, and slick as a mink's prick, Time thrusts through
      the time of no-Time.

XIX
READING LATE AT NIGHT,
THERMOMETER FALLING

[1]

The radiator's last hiss and steam-clang done, he,
Under the bare hundred-watt bulb that glares
Like truth, blanket
Over knees, woolly gray bathrobe over shoulders, handkerchief
On great bald skull spread, glasses
Low on big nose, sits. The book
Is propped on the blanket.

Thus—
But only in my mind's eye now:

and there, in the merciless
Glitter of starlight, the fields, mile
On mile over the county, stretch out and are
Crusted with ice which, whitely,
Answers the glitter of stars.

The mercury
Falls, the night is windless, mindless, and long, and somewhere,
Deep in the blackness of woods, the tendons
Of a massive oak bough snap with the sound of a
Pistol-shot.

A beam,
Somewhere in the colding house where he sits,
Groans. But his eyes do not lift. Who,
Long back, had said to me:

"When I was young I felt like I
Had to try to understand how things are, before I died."

But lived long.

                    Lived
Into that purity of being that may
Be had past all ambition and the frivolous hope, but who now
Lives only in my mind's eye,
                              though I

Cannot see what book is propped there under that forever
Marching gaze—Hume's *History of England*, Roosevelt's

Winning of the West, a Greek reader,
Now Greek to him and held in his hands like a prayer, or
Some college text book, or Freud on dreams, abandoned
By one of the children. Or, even,
Coke or Blackstone, books forbidding and blackbound, and once I,
Perhaps twelve then, found an old photograph:

                                        a young man,
In black coat, high collar, and string tie, black, one hand out
To lie with authority on a big book (Coke or Blackstone?), eyes
Lifted into space.

              And into the future.

                              Which
Had not been the future. For the future
Was only his voice that, now sudden, said:

"Son, give me that!"

He took the photograph from my hand, said:

"Some kinds of foolishness a man is due to forget, son."

Tore it across. Tore
Time, and all that Time had been, across. Threw it
Into the fire. Who,
Years later, would say:
        *

"I reckon I was lucky enough to learn early that a man
can be happy in his obligations."

Later, I found the poems. Not good.

[3]
The date on the photograph: 1890.

He was very young then. And poor.

Man lives by images. They
Lean at us from the world's wall, and Time's.

[4]
Night of the falling mercury, and ice-glitter.
Drouth-night of August and the horned insect booming
At the window-screen.

Ice-field, dusty road: distance flees.

And he sits there, and I think I hear
The faint click and grind of the brain as
It translates the perception of black marks on white paper into
Truth.

Truth is all.

We must love it.

And he loved it, who once said:

"It is terrible for a man to live and not know."

Every day he walked out to the cemetery to honor his dead.
That was truth, too.

[5]
Dear Father—Sir—the "Sir" being
The sometimes disturbed recollection
Of the time when you were big, and not dead, and I
Was little, and all boys, of that time and place, automatically
Said that to their fathers, and to any other grown man,
White of course, or damned well got their blocks
Knocked off.

        So, Sir, I,
Who certainly could never have addressed you on a matter
As important as this when you were not dead, now
Address you on it for the last time, even though
Not being, after all my previous and sometimes desperate efforts,
Sure what a son can ever say to a father, even
A dead one.

        Indecipherable passion and compulsion—well,
Wouldn't it be sad to see them, of whatever
Dark root, dwindle into mere
Self-indulgence, habit, tic of the mind, or
The picking of a scab. Reality
Is hard enough to come by, but even
In its absence we need not blaspheme
It.

   Not that
You ever could, God knows. Though I,
No doubt, have, and even now
Run the risk of doing so when I say
That I live in a profound, though
Painful, gratitude to you for what
You could not help but be: i.e., yourself.

Who, aged eighty, said:

"I've failed in a lot of things, but I don't think anybody
                    can say that I didn't have guts."

Correct.
   *

And I,
In spite of my own ignorance and failures,
Have forgiven you all your virtues.

                        Even your valor.

[6]
Who, aged eighty-six, fell to the floor,
Unconscious. Two days later,
Dead. Thus they discovered your precious secret:
A prostate big as a horse-apple. Cancer, of course.

No wonder you, who had not spent a day in bed,
Or uttered a single complaint, in the fifty years of my life,
Cried out at last.

You were entitled to that. It was only normal.

[7]
So disappeared.

            Simply not there.

                        And the seasons,
Nerve-tingling heat or premonitory chill, swung
Through the year, the years swung,

                      and the past, great
Eater of dreams, secrets, and random data, and
Refrigerator of truth, moved
Down what green valley at a glacier's
Massive pace,

           moving
At a pace not to be calculated by the trivial sun, but by
A clock more unforgiving that, at
Its distance of mathematical nightmare,
Glows forever. The ice-mass, scabbed

By earth, boulders, and some strange vegetation, moves
So imperceptibly that it seems
Only more landscape.

     Until,
In late-leveling light, some lunkhead clodhopper,
The day's work done, now trudging home,
Stops.

  Stares.

    And there it is.

      It looms.

The bulk of the unnamable and de-timed beast is now visible,
Erect, in the thinly glimmering shadow of ice.

           The lunkhead
Stares.

  The beast,
From his preternatural height, unaware of
The cringe and jaw-dropped awe crouching there below, suddenly,
As if that shimmer of ice-screen had not even been there, lifts,

Into distance,

    the magisterial gaze.

 [8]
The mercury falls. Tonight snow is predicted. This,
However, is another country.

XX
FOLLY ON ROYAL STREET
BEFORE THE RAW FACE OF GOD

Drunk, drunk, drunk, amid the blaze of noon,
Irrevocably drunk, total eclipse or,
At least, almost, and in New Orleans once,
In French Town, spring,
Off the Gulf, without storm warnings out,
Burst, like a hurricane of
Camellias, sperm, cat-squalls, fish-smells, and the old
Pain of fulfillment-that-is-not-fulfillment, so
Down Royal Street—Sunday and the street
Blank as my bank account
With two checks bounced—we—
C. and M. and I, every
Man-jack skunk-drunk—
Came.

     A cat,
Gray from the purple shadow of bougainvillaea,
Fish-head in dainty jaw-clench,
Flowed fluid as thought, secret as sin, across
The street. Was gone. We,
In the shock of that sudden and glittering vacancy, rocked
On our heels.

     A cop,
Of brachycephalic head and garlic breath,
Toothpick from side of mouth and pants ass-bagged and holster low,
From eyes the color of old coffee grounds,
Regarded with imperfect sympathy
La condition humaine—
Which was sure-God what we were.

We rocked on our heels.

          At sky-height—
Whiteness ablaze in dazzle and frazzle of light like

73

A match flame in noon-glare—a gull
Kept screaming above the doomed city.
It screamed for justice against the face of God.

Raw-ringed with glory like an ulcer, God's
Raw face stared down.

And winked.

We
Mouthed out our Milton for magnificence.

For what is man without magnificence?

Delusion, delusion!

But let
Bells ring in all the churches.
Let likker, like philosophy, roar
In the skull. Passion
Is all. Even
The sleaziest.

War
Came. Among the bed-sheet Arabs, C.
Sported his gold oak leaf. Survived.
Got back. Back to the bank. But
One morning was not there. His books,
However, were in apple-pie order. His suits,
All dark, hung in the dark closet. Drawn up
In military precision, his black shoes,
Though highly polished, gave forth
No gleam in that darkness. In Mexico,
He died.

For M.,
Twenty years in the Navy. Retired,
He fishes. Long before dawn, the launch slides out.
Land lost, he cuts the engine. The launch
Lifts, falls, in the time of the sea's slow breath.

Eastward, first light is like
A knife-edge honed to steel-brightness
And laid to the horizon. Sometimes,
He comes back in with no line wet.

As for the third, the tale
Is short. But long,
How long the art, and wisdom slow!—for him who
Once rocked on his heels, hearing the gull scream,
And quoted Milton amid the blaze of noon.

INTERJECTION # 8:
OR, SOMETIMES, NIGHT

For Paul Horgan

The unsleeping principle of delight that
Declares the arc of the apple's rondure; of, equally,
A girl's thigh that, as she lies, lifts
And draws full forward in its subtly reversed curve from
Buttock bulge to the now softly closing under-knee nook; and of
The flushed dawn cumulus: the principle
That brackets, too, the breaker's crest in one
Timeless instant, glittering, between
Last upward erg and, suddenly,
Totter and boom; and that,
In a startling burst of steel-brilliant sun, makes
The lone snow-flake dance—
                                        this principle is what,
Intermittently at least and at unlikely moments,
Comes into my mind,
Whether by day or, sometimes, night.

XXI
SUNSET WALK IN THAW-TIME IN VERMONT

1.

Rip, whoosh, wing-whistle: and out of
The spruce thicket, beating the snow from
Black spruce boughs, it
Bursts. The great partridge cock, black against flame-red,
Into the red sun of sunset, plunges. Is
Gone.

      In the ensuing
Silence, abrupt in
Back-flash and shiver of that sharp startlement, I
Stand. Stare. In mud-streaked snow,
My feet are. I,
Eyes fixed past black spruce boughs on the red west, hear,
In my chest, as from a dark cave of
No-Time, the heart
Beat.

      Where
Have the years gone?

2.

All day the stream, thaw-flooding, foamed down its gorge.
Now, skyless but for the high-tangled spruce night, it
Moves, and the bulge and slick twining of muscular water, foam-
Slashed and white-tettered, glints now only in
The cold, self-generating light of snow
Strong yet in the darkness of rock-banks.

                  The boulder
Groans in the stream, the stream heaves
In the deep certainty of its joy, like
Doom, and I,
Eyes fixed yet on the red west, begin to hear—though

Slow and numb as upon waking—
The sound of water that moves in darkness.

I stand, and in my imagination see
The slick heave of water, blacker than basalt, and on it
The stern glint, like steel, of snow-darkness.

3.

On the same spot in summer, at thrush-hour, I,
As the last light fails, have heard that full
Shadow-shimmered and deep-glinting liquidity, and
Again will; but not now.

Now

Here stare westward, and hear only
The movement of darkening water, and from
Whatever depth of being I am, ask
To be made worthy of my human failures and folly, and
Worthy of my human ignorance and anguish, and of
What soul-stillness may be achieved as I
Stand here with the cold exhalation of snow
Coiling high as my knees.

Meanwhile,

On the mountain's east hump, darkness coagulates, and
Already, where sun has not touched for hours, the new
Ice-crystal frames its massive geometry.

4.

When my son is an old man, and I have not,
For some fifty years, seen his face, and, if seeing it,
Would not even be able to guess what name it wore, what
Blessing should I ask for him?

That some time, in thaw-season, at dusk, standing
At woodside and staring
Red-westward, with the sound of moving water

In his ears, he
Should thus, in that future moment, bless,
Forward into that future's future,
An old man who, as he is mine, had once
Been his small son.

For what blessing may a man hope for but
An immortality in
The loving vigilance of death?

XXII
BIRTH OF LOVE

Season late, day late, sun just down, and the sky
Cold gunmetal but with a wash of live rose, and she,
From water the color of sky except where
Her motion has fractured it to shivering splinters of silver,
Rises. Stands on the raw grass. Against
The new-curdling night of spruces, nakedness
Glimmers and, at bosom and flank, drips
With fluent silver. The man,

Some ten strokes out, but now hanging
Motionless in the gunmetal water, feet
Cold with the coldness of depth, all
History dissolving from him, is
Nothing but an eye. Is an eye only. Sees

The body that is marked by his use, and Time's,
Rise, and in the abrupt and unsustaining element of air,
Sway, lean, grapple the pond-bank. Sees
How, with that posture of female awkwardness that is,
And is the stab of, suddenly perceived grace, breasts bulge down in
The pure curve of their weight and buttocks

Moon up and, in that swelling unity,
Are silver, and glimmer. Then

The body is erect, she is herself, whatever
Self she may be, and with an end of the towel grasped in each hand,
Slowly draws it back and forth across back and buttocks, but
With face lifted toward the high sky, where
The over-wash of rose color now fails. Fails, though no star
Yet throbs there. The towel, forgotten,
Does not move now. The gaze
Remains fixed on the sky. The body,

Profiled against the darkness of spruces, seems
To draw to itself, and condense in its whiteness, what light
In the sky yet lingers or, from
The metallic and abstract severity of water, lifts. The body,
With the towel now trailing loose from one hand, is
A white stalk from which the face flowers gravely toward the high sky.
This moment is non-sequential and absolute, and admits
Of no definition, for it
Subsumes all other, and sequential, moments, by which
Definition might be possible. The woman,

Face yet raised, wraps,
With a motion as though standing in sleep,
The towel about her body, under the breasts, and,
Holding it there, hieratic as lost Egypt and erect,
Moves up the path that, stair-steep, winds
Into the clamber and tangle of growth. Beyond
The lattice of dusk-dripping leaves, whiteness
Dimly glimmers, goes. Glimmers and is gone, and the man,

Suspended in his darkling medium, stares
Upward where, though not visible, he knows
She moves, and in his heart he cries out that, if only
He had such strength, he would put his hand forth
And maintain it over her to guard, in all
Her out-goings and in-comings, from whatever
Inclemency of sky or slur of the world's weather

Might ever be. In his heart
He cries out. Above

Height of the spruce-night and heave of the far mountain, he sees
The first star pulse into being. It gleams there.

I do not know what promise it makes to him.

XXIII
A PROBLEM IN SPATIAL COMPOSITION

[1]
Through the high window, upright rectangle of distance:

Over the green interstices and shambling glory, yet bright, of forest,
Distance flees westward, the sun low.

Beyond the distance of forest, hangs that which is blue:
Which is, in knowledge, a tall scarp of stone, gray, but now is,
In the truth of perception, stacked like a mass of blue cumulus.
Blue deepens.

What we know, we know, and
Sun now down, flame, above blue, dies upward forever in
Saffron: pure, pure and forever, the sky
Upward is. The lintel of the high window, by interruption,

Confirms what the heart knows: *beyond is forever*—

and nothing moves
Across the glister of saffron, and under the
Window the brook that,
After lalling and lounging daylong by shallow and reach,
Through dapple to glitter, now recessed in
Its premature leaf-night, utters a deeper-toned meditation.

[2]
While out of the green, up-shining ramshackle of leaf, set
In the lower right foreground, the stub
Of a great tree, gaunt-blasted and black, thrusts.

                        A single
Arm jags upward, higher goes, and in that perspective, higher
Than even the dream-blue of distance that is
The mountain.

      Then
Stabs, black, at the infinite saffron of sky.

All is ready.

     The hawk,
Entering the composition at the upper left frame
Of the window, glides,
In the pellucid ease of thought and at
His breathless angle,
Down.

    Breaks speed.

       Hangs with a slight lift and hover.

              Makes contact.

The hawk perches on the topmost, indicative tip of
The bough's sharp black and skinny jag skyward.

[3]
The hawk, in an eyeblink, is gone.

 AUDUBON
A Vision

To Allen and Helen Tate

*Thou tellest my wanderings: put thou my tears
into thy bottle: are they not in thy book?*
—PSALMS: 56, 8

*I caught at his strict shadow and the shadow
released itself with neither haste nor anger. But
he remained silent.*

—CARLOS DRUMMOND DE ANDRADE:
"TRAVELLING IN THE FAMILY"
TRANSLATED BY ELIZABETH BISHOP

Jean Jacques Audubon, whose name was anglicized when, in his youth, he was sent to America, was early instructed in the official version of his identity: that he was the son of the sea captain Jean Audubon and a first wife, who died shortly after his birth in Santo Domingo, and that the woman who brought him up in France was a second wife. Actually, he was the son of Jean Audubon and his mistress during the period when Jean Audubon was a merchant and slave-dealer in Santo Domingo, and the woman who raised him was the wife his father had left behind him in France while he was off making his fortune. By the age of ten Audubon knew the true story, but prompted, it would seem, by a variety of impulses, including some sound practical ones, he encouraged the other version, along with a number of flattering embellishments. He was, indeed, a fantasist of talent, but even without his help legends accreted about him. The most famous one—that he was the lost Dauphin of France, the son of the feckless Louis XVI and Marie Antoinette—did not, in fact, enter the picture until after his death, in 1851.

I
WAS NOT THE LOST DAUPHIN

[A]
Was not the lost dauphin, though handsome was only
Base-born and not even able
To make a decent living, was only
Himself, Jean Jacques, and his passion—what
Is man but his passion?

Saw,
Eastward and over the cypress swamp, the dawn,
Redder than meat, break;
And the large bird,
Long neck outthrust, wings crooked to scull air, moved
In a slow calligraphy, crank, flat, and black against
The color of God's blood spilt, as though
Pulled by a string.

Saw
It proceed across the inflamed distance.

Moccasins set in hoar frost, eyes fixed on the bird,
Thought: "On that sky it is black."
Thought: "In my mind it is white."
Thinking: "*Ardea occidentalis*, heron, the great one."

Dawn: his heart shook in the tension of the world.

Dawn: and what is your passion?

[B]
October: and the bear,
Daft in the honey-light, yawns.

The bear's tongue, pink as a baby's, out-crisps to the curled tip,
It bleeds the black blood of the blueberry.
        *

The teeth are more importantly white
Than has ever been imagined.

The bear feels his own fat
Sweeten, like a drowse, deep to the bone.

Bemused, above the fume of ruined blueberries,
The last bee hums.

The wings, like mica, glint
In the sunlight.

He leans on his gun. Thinks
How thin is the membrane between himself and the world.

II
THE DREAM HE NEVER KNEW THE END OF

[A]
Shank-end of day, spit of snow, the call,
A crow, sweet in distance, then sudden
The clearing: among stumps, ruined cornstalks yet standing, the spot
Like a wound rubbed raw in the vast pelt of the forest.   There
Is the cabin, a huddle of logs with no calculation or craft:
The human filth, the human hope.

                       Smoke,
From the mud-and-stick chimney, in that air, greasily
Brims, cannot lift, bellies the ridgepole, ravels
White, thin, down the shakes, like sputum.

                         He stands,
Leans on his gun, stares at the smoke, thinks: "Punk-wood."
Thinks: "Dead-fall half-rotten."   Too sloven,
That is, to even set axe to clean wood.
    *

                                                His foot,
On the trod mire by the door, crackles
The night-ice already there forming.   His hand
Lifts, hangs.   In imagination, his nostrils already
Know the stench of that lair beyond
The door-puncheons.   The dog
Presses its head against his knee.   The hand
Strikes wood.   No answer.   He halloos.   Then the voice.

     [B]
What should he recognize?   The nameless face
In the dream of some pre-dawn cock-crow—about to say what,
Do what?   The dregs
Of all nightmare are the same, and we call it
Life.   He knows that much, being a man,
And knows that the dregs of all life are nightmare.

Unless.

Unless what?

     [C]
The face, in the air, hangs.   Large,
Raw-hewn, strong-beaked, the haired mole
Near the nose, to the left, and the left side by firelight
Glazed red, the right in shadow, and under the tumble and tangle
Of dark hair on that head, and under the coarse eyebrows,
The eyes, dark, glint as from the unspecifiable
Darkness of a cave.   It is a woman.

She is tall, taller than he.
Against the gray skirt, her hands hang.

"Ye wants to spend the night?   Kin ye pay?
Well, mought as well stay then, done got one a-ready,
And leastwise, ye don't stink like no Injun."

[D]
The Indian,
Hunched by the hearth, lifts his head, looks up, but
From one eye only, the other
An aperture below which blood and mucus hang, thickening slow.

"Yeah, a arrow jounced back off his bowstring.
Durn fool—and him a Injun." She laughs.

                                    The Indian's head sinks.
So he turns, drops his pack in a corner on bearskin, props
The gun there. Comes back to the fire. Takes his watch out.
Draws it bright, on the thong-loop, from under his hunter's-frock.
It is gold, it lives in his hand in the firelight, and the woman's
Hand reaches out. She wants it. She hangs it about her neck.

And near it the great hands hover delicately
As though it might fall, they quiver like moth-wings, her eyes
Are fixed downward, as though in shyness, on that gleam, and her face
Is sweet in an outrage of sweetness, so that
His gut twists cold. He cannot bear what he sees.

Her body sways like a willow in spring wind. Like a girl.

The time comes to take back the watch. He takes it.
And as she, sullen and sunken, fixes the food, he becomes aware
That the live eye of the Indian is secretly on him, and soundlessly
The lips move, and when her back is turned, the Indian
Draws a finger, in delicious retardation, across his own throat.

After food, and scraps for his dog, he lies down:
In the corner, on bearskins, which are not well cured,
And stink, the gun by his side, primed and cocked.

Under his hand he feels the breathing of the dog.

The woman hulks by the fire. He hears the jug slosh.

[E]
The sons come in from the night, two, and are
The sons she would have. Through slit lids
He watches. Thinks: "Now."

The sons
Hunker down by the fire, block the firelight, cram food
Into their large mouths, where teeth
Grind in the hot darkness, their breathing
Is heavy like sleep, he wants to sleep, but
The head of the woman leans at them. The heads
Are together in firelight.

He hears the jug slosh.

Then hears,
Like the whisper and *whish* of silk, that other
Sound, like a sound of sleep, but he does not
Know what it is. Then knows, for,
Against firelight, he sees the face of the woman
Lean over, and the lips purse sweet as to bestow a kiss, but
This is not true, and the great glob of spit
Hangs there, glittering, before she lets it fall.

The spit is what softens like silk the passage of steel
On the fine-grained stone. It whispers.

When she rises, she will hold it in her hand.

[F]
With no sound, she rises. She holds it in her hand.
Behind her the sons rise like shadow. The Indian
Snores. Or pretends to.

He thinks: "Now."

And knows

He has entered the tale, knows
He has entered the dark hovel

In the forest where trees have eyes, knows it is the tale
They told him when he was a child, knows it
Is the dream he had in childhood but never
Knew the end of, only
The scream.

　　[G]
But no scream now, and under his hand
The dog lies taut, waiting.　And he, too, knows
What he must do, do soon, and therefore
Does not understand why now a lassitude
Sweetens his limbs, or why, even in this moment
Of fear—or is it fear?—the saliva
In his mouth tastes sweet.

"Now, now!" the voice in his head cries out, but
Everything seems far away, and small.

He cannot think what guilt unmans him, or
Why he should find the punishment so precious.

It is too late.　Oh, oh, the world!

Tell me the name of the world.

　　[H]
The door bursts open, and the travelers enter:
Three men, alert, strong, armed.　And the Indian
Is on his feet, pointing.

　　　　　　　He thinks
That now he will never know the dream's ending.

　　[I]
Trussed up with thongs, all night they lie on the floor there.
The woman is gagged, for she had reviled them.
All night he hears the woman's difficult breath.
　　*

Dawn comes. It is gray. When he eats,
The cold corn pone grinds in his throat, like sand. It sticks there.

Even whiskey fails to remove it. It sticks there.

The leg-thongs are cut off the tied-ones. They are made to stand up.
The woman refuses the whiskey. Says: "What fer?"
The first son drinks. The other
Takes it into his mouth, but it will not go down.

The liquid drains, slow, from the slack side of the mouth.

    [J]
They stand there under the long, low bough of the great oak.
Eastward, low over the forest, the sun is nothing
But a circular blur of no irradiation, somewhat paler
Then the general grayness. Their legs
Are again bound with thongs.

They are asked if they want to pray now. But the woman:
"If'n it's God made folks, then who's to pray to?"
And then: "Or fer?" And bursts into laughing.

For a time it seems that she can never stop laughing.

But as for the sons, one prays, or tries to. And one
Merely blubbers. If the woman
Gives either a look, it is not
Pity, nor even contempt, only distance. She waits,

And is what she is,

And in the gray light of morning, he sees her face. Under
The tumbled darkness of hair, the face
Is white. Out of that whiteness
The dark eyes stare at nothing, or at
The nothingness that the gray sky, like Time, is, for
There is no Time, and the face
Is, he suddenly sees, beautiful as stone, and
    *

So becomes aware that he is in the manly state.

    [K]

The affair was not tidy: bough low, no drop, with the clients
Simply hung up, feet not much clear of the ground, but not
Quite close enough to permit any dancing.
The affair was not quick: both sons long jerking and farting, but she,
From the first, without motion, frozen
In a rage of will, an ecstasy of iron, as though
This was the dream that, lifelong, she had dreamed toward.

                                         The face,

Eyes a-glare, jaws clenched, now glowing black with congestion
Like a plum, had achieved,
It seemed to him, a new dimension of beauty.

    [L]

There are tears in his eyes.
He tries to remember his childhood.
He tries to remember his wife.
He can remember nothing.

His throat is parched. His right hand,
Under the deerskin frock, has been clutching the gold watch.

The magic of that object had been,
In the secret order of the world, denied her who now hangs there.

He thinks: "What has been denied me?"
Thinks: "There is never an answer."

Thinks: "The question is the only answer."

He yearns to be able to frame a definition of joy.

    [M]

And so stood alone, for the travelers

Had disappeared into the forest and into
Whatever selves they were, and the Indian,
Now bearing the gift of a gun that had belonged to the hanged-ones,
Was long since gone, like smoke fading into the forest,
And below the blank and unforgiving eye-hole
The blood and mucus had long since dried.

He thought: "I must go."

                            But could not, staring
At the face, and stood for a time even after
The first snowflakes, in idiotic benignity,
Had fallen. Far off, in the forest and falling snow,
A crow was calling.

                        So stirs, knowing now
He will not be here when snow
Drifts into the open door of the cabin, or,
Descending the chimney, mantles thinly
Dead ashes on the hearth, nor when snow thatches
These heads with white, like wisdom, nor ever will he
Hear the infinitesimal stridor of the frozen rope
As wind shifts its burden, or when

The weight of the crow first comes to rest on a rigid shoulder.

III
WE ARE ONLY OURSELVES

We never know what we have lost, or what we have found.
We are only ourselves, and that promise.
Continue to walk in the world.   Yes, love it!

He continued to walk in the world.

IV
THE SIGN WHEREBY HE KNEW

[A]
His life, at the end, seemed—even the anguish—simple.
Simple, at least, in that it had to be,
Simply, what it was, as he was,
In the end, himself and not what
He had known he ought to be.   The blessedness!—

To wake in some dawn and see,
As though down a rifle barrel, lined up
Like sights, the self that was, the self that is, and there,
Far off but in range, completing that alignment, your fate.

Hold your breath, let the trigger-squeeze be slow and steady.

The quarry lifts, in the halo of gold leaves, its noble head.

This is not a dimension of Time.

[B]
In this season the waters shrink.

The spring is circular and surrounded by gold leaves
Which are fallen from the beech tree.

Not even a skitter-bug disturbs the gloss
Of the surface tension.   The sky

Is reflected below in absolute clarity.
If you stare into the water you may know

That nothing disturbs the infinite blue of the sky.

[C]
Keep store, dandle babies, and at night nuzzle
The hazelnut-shaped sweet tits of Lucy, and
With the piratical mark-up of the frontier, get rich.

But you did not, being of weak character.

You saw, from the forest pond, already dark, the great trumpeter swan
Rise, in clangor, and fight up the steep air where,
At the height of last light, it glimmered, like white flame.

The definition of love being, as we know, complex,
We may say that he, after all, loved his wife.

The letter, from campfire, keelboat, or slum room in New Orleans,
Always ended, "God bless you, dear Lucy." After sunset,

Alone, he played his flute in the forest.

[D]
Listen! Stand very still and,
Far off, where shadow
Is undappled, you may hear

The tusked boar grumble in his ivy-slick.

Afterward, there is silence until
The jay, sudden as conscience, calls.

The call, in the infinite sunlight, is like
The thrill of the taste of—on the tongue—brass.

[E]
The world declares itself. That voice
Is vaulted in—oh, arch on arch—redundancy of joy, its end
Is its beginning, necessity
Blooms like a rose. Why,
        *

Therefore, is truth the only thing that cannot
Be spoken?

It can only be enacted, and that in dream,
Or in the dream become, as though unconsciously, action, and he stood,

At dusk, in the street of the raw settlement, and saw
The first lamp lit behind a window, and did not know
What he was. Thought: "I do not know my own name."

He walked in the world. He was sometimes seen to stand
In perfect stillness, when no leaf stirred.

Tell us, dear God—tell us the sign
Whereby we may know the time has come.

V
THE SOUND OF THAT WIND

[A]
He walked in the world. Knew the lust of the eye.

Wrote: "Ever since a Boy I have had an astonishing desire
            to see Much of the World and particularly
            to acquire a true knowledge of the Birds of North America."

He dreamed of hunting with Boone, from imagination painted his portrait.
He proved that the buzzard does not scent its repast, but sights it.
He looked in the eye of the wounded white-headed eagle.

Wrote: ". . . the Noble Fellow looked at his Ennemies
            with a Contemptible Eye."

At dusk he stood on a bluff, and the bellowing of buffalo
Was like distant ocean. He saw

Bones whiten the plain in the hot daylight.

He saw the Indian, and felt the splendor of God.

Wrote: "... for there I see the Man Naked from his
hand and yet free from acquired Sorrow."

Below the salt, in rich houses, he sat, and knew insult.
In the lobbies and couloirs of greatness he dangled,
And was not unacquainted with contumely.

Wrote: "My Lovely Miss Pirrie of Oackley Passed by Me
this Morning, but did not remember how beautifull
I had rendered her face once by Painting it
at her Request with Pastelles."

Wrote: "... but thanks to My humble talents I can run
the gantlet throu this World without her help."

And ran it, and ran undistracted by promise of ease,
Nor even the kind condescension of Daniel Webster.

Wrote: "... would give me a fat place was I willing to
have one; but I love indepenn and piece more
than humbug and money."

And proved same, but in the end, entered
On honor. Far, over the ocean, in the silken salons,
With hair worn long like a hunter's, eyes shining,
He whistled the bird-calls of his distant forest.

Wrote: "... in my sleep I continually dream of birds."

And in the end, entered into his earned house,
And slept in a bed, and with Lucy.

                           But the fiddle
Soon lay on the shelf untouched, the mouthpiece
Of the flute was dry, and his brushes.
        *

                              His mind
Was darkened, and his last joy
Was in the lullaby they sang him, in Spanish, at sunset.

He died, and was mourned, who had loved the world.

Who had written: ". . . a world which though wicked enough
                          in all conscience is *perhaps* as good
                          as worlds unknown."

        [B]
So died in his bed, and
Night leaned, and now leans,
Off the Atlantic, and is on schedule.
Grass does not bend beneath that enormous weight
That with no sound sweeps westward.   In the Mississippi,
On a mud bank, the wreck of a great tree, left
By flood, lies, the root-system and now-stubbed boughs
Lifting in darkness.   It
Is white as bone.   That whiteness
Is reflected in dark water, and a star
Thereby.

            Later,
In the shack of a sheep-herder, high above the Bitterroot,
The light goes out.   No other
Light is visible.

The Northwest Orient plane, New York to Seattle, has passed,
                                          winking westward.

        [C]
For everything there is a season.

But there is the dream
Of a season past all seasons.
        *

In such a dream the wild-grape cluster,
High-hung, exposed in the gold light,
Unripening, ripens.

Stained, the lip with wetness gleams.

I see your lip, undrying, gleam in the bright wind.

I cannot hear the sound of that wind.

VI
LOVE AND KNOWLEDGE

Their footless dance
Is of the beautiful liability of their nature.
Their eyes are round, boldly convex, bright as a jewel,
And merciless.   They do not know
Compassion, and if they did,
We should not be worthy of it.   They fly
In air that glitters like fluent crystal
And is hard as perfectly transparent iron, they cleave it
With no effort.   They cry
In a tongue multitudinous, often like music.

He slew them, at surprising distances, with his gun.
Over a body held in his hand, his head was bowed low,
But not in grief.

He put them where they are, and there we see them:
In our imagination.

What is love?

One name for it is knowledge.

VII
TELL ME A STORY

[A]
Long ago, in Kentucky, I, a boy, stood
By a dirt road, in first dark, and heard
The great geese hoot northward.

I could not see them, there being no moon
And the stars sparse. I heard them.

I did not know what was happening in my heart.

It was the season before the elderberry blooms,
Therefore they were going north.

The sound was passing northward.

[B]
Tell me a story.

In this century, and moment, of mania,
Tell me a story.

Make it a story of great distances, and starlight.

The name of the story will be Time,
But you must not pronounce its name.

Tell me a story of deep delight.

from
INCARNATIONS
Poems 1966-1968

To John Palmer

Yet now our flesh is as the flesh of our brethren.
—NEHEMIAH: 5,5

John Henry said to the Captain, "A man ain't nuthin but a man."
—A FOLK BALLAD

I
Island of Summer

ISLAND OF SUMMER

1
WHAT DAY IS

In Pliny, *Phoenice*. Phoenicians,
Of course. Before that, Celts.
Rome, in the end, as always:
A handful of coins, a late emperor.
Hewn stone, footings for what?
Irrigation, but now not easy
To trace a flume-line.

                Later,
Monks, Moors, murderers,
The Mediterranean flotsam, not
Excluding the English, they cut
Down olives, plucked vines up, burnt
The chateau.

             All day, cicadas,
At the foot of infinity, like
A tree, saw. The sawdust
Of that incessant effort,
Like filings of brass, sun-brilliant,
Heaps up at the tree-foot. That
Is what day is.

           Do not
Look too long at the sea, for
That brightness will rinse out your eyeballs.

They will go gray as dead moons.

WHERE THE SLOW FIG'S PURPLE SLOTH

Where the slow fig's purple sloth
Swells, I sit and meditate the
Nature of the soul, the fig exposes,
To the blaze of afternoon, one haunch
As purple-black as Africa, a single
Leaf the rest screens, but through it, light
Burns, and for the fig's bliss
The sun dies, the sun
Has died forever—far, oh far—
For the fig's bliss, thus.

        The air
Is motionless, and the fig,
Motionless in that imperial and blunt
Languor of glut, swells, and inward
The fibers relax like a sigh in that
Hot darkness, go soft, the air
Is gold.

     When you
Split the fig, you will see
Lifting from the coarse and purple seed, its
Flesh like flame, purer
Than blood.

     It fills
The darkening room with light.

3
NATURAL HISTORY I

Many have died here, but few
Have names, it is like the world, bodies
Have been eaten by dogs, gulls, rodents, ants,
And fish, and Messire Jean le Maingre,
He struck them, and they fled.

                            Et les Sarrasins
se retirèrent en une ile qui est devant
le dict chastel—

                    but little good that, for
The *Maréchal* was hot on them, and

                                    des leurs
y perdirent plus de quatre cent hommes,
que morts, que affolez,

                        and the root
Of the laurel has profited, the leaf
Of the live-oak achieves a new luster, the mouth
Of the mullet is agape, and my ten-year-old son,
In the island dump, finds a helmet, Nazi—from left
To right, entering at the temple, small and
Perfectly round at the point of entry, neat, but
At egress large, raw, exploding outward, desperate for
Light, air, and openness after
The hot enclosure and intense dark of
That brief transit: this
The track of the missile. Death
Came quick, for history,
Like nature, may have mercy,
Though only by accident. Neither
Has tears.

            But at dusk
From the next island, from its pad at

Le centre de recherche d'engins spécieux, the rocket
Rises, the track of fume now feathers white—spins out, oh whiter—
Rises beyond the earth's shadow, in
Full light aspires. Then,
With no sound, the expected explosion. The glitters
Of flame fall, like shreds of bright foil, ice-bright, from
A Christmas tree, die in earth's shadow, but
The feathers of fume yet hang high, dissolve
White in that last light. The technicians
Now go to dinner.

    Beauty
Is the fume-track of necessity. This thought
Is therapeutic.

    If, after several
Applications, you do not find
Relief, consult your family physician.

  4
RIDDLE IN THE GARDEN

My mind is intact, but the shapes
of the world change, the peach
has released the bough and at last
makes full confession, its *pudeur*
has departed like peach-fuzz wiped off, and

We now know how the hot sweet-
ness of flesh and the juice-dark hug
the rough peach-pit, we know its most
suicidal yearnings, it wants
to suffer extremely, it
  *

Loves God, and I warn you, do not
touch that plum, it will burn you, a blister
will be on your finger, and you will
put the finger to your lips for relief—oh, do
be careful not to break that soft

Gray bulge of fruit-skin of blister, for
exposing that inwardness will
increase your pain, for you
are part of the world. You think
I am speaking in riddles. But I am not, for

The world means only itself.

5
PAUL VALÉRY STOOD ON THE CLIFF AND CONFRONTED THE FURIOUS ENERGIES OF NATURE

Where dust gritty as
    Hot sand was hurled by
    Sea-wind on the cliff-track
    To burnish the holly-leaf, he

Walked, and white the far sail
    Heeled off from windward, and white
    Cat's paws up the channel flicked.
    He paused to look, and far down,

Surf, on the Pointe du Cognet,
    Boomed, and clawed white,
    Like vine incessant, up
    That glitter and lattice of air.

Far down, far down, below
    The stone where his foot hung, a gull

Wheeled white in the flame of
Air. The white wing scythed

The bright stalks of altitude
　　Down, they were cut at the root,
　　And the sky keeps falling down,
　　Forever it falls down with

A clatter like glass, or delight,
　　And his head, like a drum, throbs,
　　His eyes, they fly away,
　　They scream like gulls, and

Over Africa burn all night,
　　But Time is not time, therefore
　　His breath stops in his throat
　　And he stands on the cliff, his white

Panama hat in hand,
　　For he is Monsieur le Poète,
　　Paul Valéry is his name,
　　On a promenade by the sea, so

He sways high against the blue sky,
　　While in the bright intricacies
　　Of wind, his mind, like a leaf,
　　Turns. In the sun, it glitters.

6
TREASURE HUNT

Hunt, hunt again. If you do not find it, you
Will die. But I tell you this much, it
Is not under the stone at the foot
Of the garden, nor by the wall at the fig tree.

I tell you this much to save you trouble, for I
Have looked, I know. But hurry, for

The terror is, all promises are kept.

Even happiness.

7

MYTH ON MEDITERRANEAN BEACH:
APHRODITE AS LOGOS

From left to right, she leads the eye
Across the blaze-brightness of sea and sky

That is the background of her transit.

Commanded thus, from left to right,
As by a line of print on that bright

Blankness, the eye will follow, but

There is no line, the eye follows only
That one word moving, it moves in lonely

And absolute arrogance across the blank

Page of the world, the word burns, she is
The word, all faces turn. Look!—this

Is what she is: old hunchback in bikini.

A contraption of angles and bulges, an old
Robot with pince-nez and hair dyed gold,

She heaves along beneath the hump.
    *

The breasts hang down like saddle-bags,
To balance the hump the belly sags,

And under the belly-bulge, the flowers

Of the gee-string garland the private parts.
She grinds along by fits and starts

Beside the margin of the sea,

Past children and sand-castles and
The lovers strewn along the sand.

Her pince-nez glitter like contempt

For all delusion, and the French lad
Who exhibitionistically had

Been fondling the American college girl

Loses his interest. Ignoring him,
The hunchback stares at the horizon rim,

Then slowly, as compulsion grows,

She foots the first frail lace of foam
That is the threshold of her lost home,

And moved by memory in the blood,

Enters that vast indifferency
Of perfection that we call the sea.

How long, how long, she lingers there

She may not know, somnambulist
In that realm where no Time may subsist,

But in the end will again feel
             *

The need to rise and re-enact
The miracle of the human fact.

She lifts her head, looks toward the shore.

She moves toward us, abstract and slow,
And watching, we feel the slow knowledge grow—

How from the breasts the sea recedes,

How the great-gashed navel's cup
Pours forth the ichor that had filled it up.

How the wavelets sink to seek, and seek,

Then languishing, sink to lave the knees,
And lower, to kiss the feet, as these

Find the firm ground where they must go.

The last foam crisps about the feet.
She shivers, smiles. She stands complete

In Botticellian parody.

Bearing her luck upon her back,
She turns now to take the lifeward track,

And lover by lover, on she moves

Toward her own truth, and does not stop.
Each foot stumps flat with the big toe up,

But under the heel, the damp-packed sand,

With that compression, like glory glows,
And glory attends her as she goes.

In rapture now she heaves along,
  *

The pince-nez glitter at her eyes,
The flowers wreathe her moving thighs,

For she treads the track the blessèd know

To a shore far lonelier than this
Where waits her apotheosis.

She passes the lovers, one by one,

And passing, draws their dreams away,
And leaves them naked to the day.

8
THE IVY

The ivy assaults the wall. The ivy
    says: "I will pull you down." Time
    is nothing to the ivy. The ivy

Does not sweat at night, for like the sea
    it dreams a single dream, it
    is its own dream. Therefore,

Peace is the dream's name. The wall
    is stone, and all night the stone,
    where no stars may come, dreams.

Night comes. You sleep. What is your dream?

9
WHERE PURPLES NOW THE FIG

Where purples now the fig, flame in
    Its inmost flesh, a leaf hangs
    Down, and on it, gull-droppings, white
    As chalk, show, for the sun has

Burned all white, for the sun, it would
    Burn our bones to chalk—yes, keep
    Them covered, oh flesh, oh sweet
    Integument, oh frail, depart not

And leave me thus exposed, like Truth.

10
THE RED MULLET

The fig flames inward on the bough, and I,
Deep where the great mullet, red, lounges in
Black shadow of the shoal, have come. Where no light may

Come, he the great one, like flame, burns, and I
Have met him, eye to eye, the lower jaw horn,
Outthrust, arched down at the corners, merciless as

Genghis, motionless and mogul, and the eye of
The mullet is round, bulging, ringed like a target
In gold, vision is armor, he sees and does not

Forgive. The mullet has looked me in the eye, and forgiven
Nothing. At night I fear suffocation, is there
Enough air in the world for us all, therefore I
    *

Swim much, dive deep to develop my lung-case, I am
Familiar with the agony of will in the deep place. Blood
Thickens as oxygen fails. Oh, mullet, thy flame

Burns in the shadow of the black shoal.

11
A PLACE WHERE NOTHING IS

I have been in a place where
nothing is, it is not
silence, for there are voices, not
emptiness, for there is
a great fullness, it is
populated with nothingness, nothing-
ness presses on the ribs like
elbows angry, and the lump
of nothingness sticks
in the throat like the hard
phlegm, and if, in that dark,
you cough, there is, in that
land of nothingness, no
echo, for the dark has
no walls, or if there is echo,
it is, whatever the original
sound, a laugh. A lamp
by each bed burns, but
gives no light.

       Earlier,
I have warned you not to look
too long at the brightness of
the sea, but now—yes—
I retract my words, for
the brightness of that nothing-

ness which is the sea is
not nothingness, but is
like the inestimable sea of

Nothingness Plotinus dreamed.

12
MASTS AT DAWN

Past second cock-crow yacht masts in the harbor go slowly white.

No light in the east yet, but the stars show a certain fatigue.
They withdraw into a new distance, have discovered our
                                        unworthiness. It is long since

The owl, in the dark eucalyptus, dire and melodious, last called, and

Long since the moon sank and the English
Finished fornicating in their ketches. In the evening
                                there was a strong swell.

Red died the sun, but at dark wind rose easterly, white
                        sea nagged the black harbor headland.

When there is a strong swell, you may, if you surrender to it, experience
A sense, in the act, of mystic unity with that rhythm. Your peace
                                is the sea's will.

But now no motion, the bay-face is glossy in darkness, like

An old window pane flat on black ground by the wall, near
                                the ash heap. It neither
Receives nor gives light. Now is the hour when the sea

Sinks into meditation. It doubts its own mission. The drowned cat
    *

That on the evening swell had kept nudging the piles of
                                        the pier and had seemed
To want to climb out and lick itself dry, now floats free. On that
                                surface a slight convexity only, it is like

An eyelid, in darkness, closed. You must learn to accept the
                                        kiss of fate, for

The masts go white slow, as light, like dew, from darkness
Condenses on them, on oiled wood, on metal. Dew whitens in darkness.

I lie in my bed and think how, in darkness, the masts go white.

The sound of the engine of the first fishing dory dies seaward. Soon
In the inland glen wakes the dawn-dove. We must try

To love so well the world that we may believe, in the end, in God.

13
THE LEAF

[A]
Here the fig lets down the leaf, the leaf
Of the fig five fingers has, the fingers
Are broad, spatulate, stupid,
Ill-formed, and innocent—but of a hand, and the hand,

To hide me from the blaze of the wide world, drops,
Shamefast, down. I am
What is to be concealed. I lurk
In the shadow of the fig. Stop.
Go no further. This is the place.

To this spot I bring my grief.
Human grief is the obscenity to be hidden by the leaf.

[B]
We have undergone ourselves, therefore
What more is to be done for Truth's sake? I

Have watched the deployment of ants, I
Have conferred with the flaming mullet in a deep place.

Near the nesting place of the hawk, among
Snag-rock, high on the cliff, I have seen
The clutter of annual bones, of hare, vole, bird, white
As chalk from sun and season, frail
As the dry grass stem. On that

High place of stone I have lain down, the sun
Beat, the small exacerbation
Of dry bones was what my back, shirtless and bare, knew. I saw

The hawk shudder in the high sky, he shudders
To hold position in the blazing wind, in relation to
The firmament, he shudders and the world is a metaphor, his eye
Sees, white, the flicker of hare-scut, the movement of vole.

Distance is nothing, there is no solution, I
Have opened my mouth to the wind of the world like wine, I wanted
To taste what the world is, wind dried up

The live saliva of my tongue, my tongue
Was like a dry leaf in my mouth.

Destiny is what you experience, that
Is its name and definition, and is your name, for

The wide world lets down the hand in shame:
Here is the human shadow, there, of the wide world, the flame.

[C]
The world is fruitful. In this heat
The plum, black yet bough-bound, bursts, and the gold ooze is,
Of bees, joy, the gold ooze has striven

Outward, it wants again to be of
The goldness of air and—blessèdly—innocent. The grape
Weakens at the juncture of the stem. The world

Is fruitful, and I, too,
In that I am the father
Of my father's father's father. I,
Of my father, have set the teeth on edge. But
By what grape? I have cried out in the night.

From a further garden, from the shade of another tree,
My father's voice, in the moment when the cicada

                                        ceases, has called to me.

     [D]
The voice blesses me for the only
Gift I have given: *teeth set on edge.*

In the momentary silence of the cicada,
I can hear the appalling speed,
In space beyond stars, of
Light. It is

A sound like wind.

II

Internal Injuries

PENOLOGICAL STUDY:
SOUTHERN EXPOSURE

To Brainard and Frances Cheney

1
KEEP THAT MORPHINE MOVING, CAP

Oh, in the pen, oh, in the pen,
The cans, they have no doors, therefore
I saw him, head bent in that primordial
Prayer, head grizzled, and the sweat,
To the gray cement, dropped. It dripped,
And each drop glittered as it fell,
For in the pen, oh, in the pen,
The cans, they have no doors.

Each drop upon that gray cement
Exploded like a star, and the Warden,
I heard the Warden saying, "Jake—
You know we're pulling for you, Jake,"
And I saw that face lift and explode
In whiteness like a star, for oh!—
Oh, in the pen, yes, in the pen,
The cans, they have no doors.

A black hole opened in that white
That was the star-exploding face,
And words came out, the words came out,
"Jest keep that morphine moving, Cap,
And me, I'll tough it through,"
Who had toughed it through nigh forty years,
And couldn't now remember why
He had cut her throat that night, and so

Come to the pen, here to the pen,
Where cans, they have no doors,

And where he sits, while deep inside,
Inside his gut, inside his gut,
The pumpkin grows and grows, and only
In such a posture humped, can he
Hold tight his gut, and half believe,
Like you or me, like you or me,
That the truth will not be true.—Oh, Warden,

Keep that morphine moving, for
All night beneath that blazing bulb,
Bright drop by drop, from the soaked hair, sweat
Drips, and each drop, on the gray cement
Explodes like a star. Listen to that
Small sound, and let us, too, keep pulling
For him, like we all ought to, who,
When truth at last is true, must try,
Like him, to tough it through—but no!—
Not in the pen, not in the pen,
Where cans, they have no doors.

2
TOMORROW MORNING

In the morning the rivers will blaze up blue like sulphur.
Even the maps will shrivel black in their own heat,
And metaphors will scream in the shared glory of their referents.
Truth will embrace you with tentacles like an octopus. It
Will suck your blood through a thousand suction-cups, and
The sun utter the intolerable trill of a flame-martyred canary.

Does this suggest the beginning of a new life for us all?
        *

Or is it only, as I have heard an eminent physician remark,
A characteristic phase at the threshold of the final narcosis?

WET HAIR: IF NOW HIS MOTHER SHOULD COME

If out of a dire suspicion
She hadn't touched his hair and
Found it yet damp at the roots, she might
Have forgiven the fact he was late,
With supper near over now, and the lamp

On the table already lighted, and shadows
Bigger than people and blacker than niggers swinging
On the board walls of the kitchen, one kid,
The youngest, already asleep,
The head at the edge of
The plate, and tighter than glue
In that hot night, one cheek
To the checked oil-cloth table cover, and grease
Gone gray on the forks—yes, if

She hadn't then touched his hair,
She might never have guessed how he'd been in
That durn creek again, and then lied,
And so might never have fetched him that
Awful whack. His face

In the lamplight was white. She

Stood there and heard how,
Maniacal and incessant,
Out in the dark, the
Insects of summer tore
The night to shreds. She

Stood there and tried to think she
Was somebody else. But
Wasn't, so

Put him to bed without supper.

What if tonight when
Again the insects of summer
Are tearing the night to shreds, she
Should come to this room where under the blazing
Bulb, sweat drips, and each drop,
On that gray cement, explodes like
A star? What if she
Should touch his head and now
Find the hair wetter than ever?

I do not think that now she
Would fetch him that awful
Whack—even if

Again he had come late to supper,
Then lied, to boot.

4
NIGHT: THE MOTEL DOWN THE ROAD
FROM THE PEN

Now in the cheap motel, I lie, and
Belly-up, the dead catfish slides
All night glimmering down the river
That is black and glossy as
Old oil bleeding soundlessly
From the crank-case. Look! the stars
*

Are there, they shine, and the river
Knows their white names as it flows,
And white in starlight the white belly
Glimmers down the magisterial
Moving night the river is.

In this motel, I lie and sweat.
It is summer, it is summer.

The river moves. It does not stop.
It, like night, is going somewhere.

It is going, somewhere.

5

WHERE THEY COME TO WAIT FOR THE BODY:
A GHOST STORY

This is the cheap motel where
They come to wait for the body if they
Are white, and have three dollars to spare,

Which is tough if you had to scrape up to pay
Private for the undertaker because you
Hope he'll make things look better some way,

But won't, for with twenty-three hundred volts gone through,
The customer's not John Barrymore,
And the face he's got will just have to do

Him on out, so load the finished product and go, for
You've long since done with your crying, and now
It's like it all happened long back, or
        *

To somebody else. But referring to Jake, how
Could they schedule delivery, it might be next week,
Or might, if things broke right, be even tomorrow,

But who gives a damn how the cheese, so to speak,
Gets sliced, for nobody's waiting to haul
Jake back to any home cross-roads or creek,

And there's nobody here, nobody at all,
Who knows his name even, but me, and I know
Only the Jake part, but I've got a call

In for five A.M., for I'm due to blow
At half-past, but if he'd be checked out and ready,
If that's not too early for him, he can go

With me, and we roll, and his eyes stare moody
Down a road all different from the last time he passed,
And the new slab whirls at him white now and steady,

And what he might recognize snaps by so fast
That hill and stream and field all blur
To a misty glitter, till at last

He shifts on his hams and his stiff hands stir
On his knees, and he says: "That bluff—thar 'tis!
Jest let me off thar, thank you kindly, sir."

And so he drops off at the creek where that bluff is,
And the shadow of woods spills down to the bone-
White slab, and with back to the screech and whizz

Of the traffic, he stands, like he was alone
And noise no different from silence, his face set
Woodsward and hillsward, then sudden, he's gone,

And me, I'm gone too, as I flog the U-Drive-It
Toward Nashville, where faces of friends, some dead, gleam,
And where, when the time comes, you grab the jet.

6
NIGHT IS PERSONAL

Night is personal. Day is public. Day
Is like a pair of pants you can buy anywhere, and do.

When you are through with day you hang it up like pants on
The back of a chair, and it glows all night in the motel room, but not

Enough to keep you awake. Jake is awake. Oh, Warden,
Keep that morphine moving, for we are all

One flesh, and back in your office, in the dark, the telephone
Is thinking up something to say, it is going to say

It does not love you, for night is each man's legend, and there is no joy
Without some pain. Jake is meditating his joy. He sweats. Oh, Warden,

Keep that morphine moving, for I feel something
Soft as feathers whispering in me, and

Corpuscles grind in your own blood-stream, like gravel
In a freshet, and by this sign know that a congress

Of comets will be convened screaming, they will comb their
Long hair with blue fingers cold as ice, their tears are precious, therefore

My head explodes with flowers like a gangster's funeral, but
                                        all this racket won't
Matter, for Jake is awake anyway. Oh, Warden, keep
                                that morphine moving, for

When you get home tonight your wife will be weeping. She
Will not know why, for in the multiple eye of the spider, the world bleeds

Many times over, the spider is hairy like a Jewish Jesus, it
                                        is soft like a peach
Mercilessly bruised, you have tasted the blood of the spider, and
    *

It smiles, it knows. Jake is awake. Oh, Warden,
Keep that morphine moving, for your father is not really dead, he

Is trying to get out of that box he thinks you put him in, and
                              on the floor by your bed, in the dark,
Your old dog, like conscience, sighs, the tail feebly thumps, it wants

To be friends again, it will forgive you even if now you
Do take it to the vet, for now is the time, it has suffered
                              enough. Oh, Warden,

Keep that morphine moving, for we've had a frightful summer, sweat
Stings my eyes, salt pills do no good, forest fires rage
                              at night in the mountains. Warden,

Things have got to change around here. Jake's case is simply
One of many. An investigation is coming, I warn you. And anyway,

Night is personal, night is personal. There are many nights, Warden,
And you have no reason to think that you are above the Law.

7
DAWN

Owl, owl, stop calling from the swamp, let
Old orange peel and condoms and
That dead catfish, belly white, and
Whitely, whitely, the shed petals
Of catalpa—let all, all,
Slide whitely down the sliding darkness
That the river is, let stars
Dip dawnward down the un-owled air, and sweat
Dry on the sheet.
        *

But

Stars now assume the last brightness, it
Is not yet dawn. Dawn will, it
Is logical to postulate, though not
Certain, come, and the sun then,
Above the horizon, burst
Like a blast of buckshot through
A stained-glass window, for

It is summer, it is summer.

Forgive us, this day, our joy.

Far off, a red tractor is crossing the black field.
Iron crushes the last dawn-tangle of ground mist.

Forgive us—oh, give us!—our joy.

INTERNAL INJURIES

1
THE EVENT

Nigger: as if it were not
Enough to be old, and a woman, to be
Poor, having a sizeable hole (as
I can plainly see, you being flat on the ground) in
The sole of a shoe (the right one), enough to be

Alone (your daughter off in
Detroit, in three years no letter, your son

Upriver in the pen, at least now you know
Where he is, and no friends), enough to be

Fired (as you have just today
Been, and unfair to boot, for
That durn Jew-lady—there wasn't no way
To know it was you that opened that there durn
Purse, just picking on you on account of
Your complexion), enough to be

Yourself (yes, after sixty-eight
Years, just to have to be
What you are, yeah, look
In the mirror, that
Is you, and when did you
Pray last), enough to be,

Merely to be—Jesus,
Wouldn't just *being* be enough without
Having to have the pee (quite
Literally) knocked out of
You by a 1957 yellow Cadillac driven by
A spic, and him
From New Jersey?

Why couldn't it of at least been a white man?

2
THE SCREAM

The scream comes as regular
As a metronome. Twelve beats
For period of scream, twelve
For period of non-scream, there
Must be some sort of clockwork

Inside you to account for such
Perfection, perhaps you have always
And altogether been clockwork, but
Not realizing its perfection, I
Had thought you merely human.

I apologize for the error, but
It was, under the circumstances,
Only natural.

                Pneumatic hammers
Are at work somewhere. In the period
Of non-scream, they seem merely a part of the silence.

3
HER HAT

They are tearing down Penn Station,
Through which joy and sorrow passed,

But against the bright blue May-sky,
In the dazzle and sun-blast,

I can see one cornice swimming
High above the boarding where

Sidewalk superintendents turn now
From their duties and at you stare,

While I, sitting in my taxi,
Watch them watching you, for I,

Ashamed of their insensitiveness,
Am no Peeping Tom with my
        *

Own face pressed directly to the
Window of your pain to peer

Deep in your inward darkness, waiting,
With slack-jawed and spit-wet leer,

For what darkling gleam, and spasm,
Visceral and pure, like love.

Look! your hat's right under a truck wheel.
It's lucky traffic can't yet move.

Somewhere—oh, somewhere above the city—a jet is prowling the sky.

4
THE ONLY TROUBLE

The only trouble was, you got up
This morning on the wrong side of the bed, and of
Your life. First, you put the wrong shoe on the right
Foot, or vice versa, and next
You quarreled with your husband. No—
You merely remembered a quarrel you had with him before he
Up and died, or did he merely blow, and never
Was rightly your husband, nohow.

                           Defect of attention
Is defect of character, and now
The scream floats up, and up, like a
Soap bubble, it is enormous, it glitters
Above the city, it is as big as the city,
And on its bottom side all the city is
Accurately reflected, making allowance
For curvature, upside-down, iridescent as
A dream—and as pale!
   *

                        If children were here now,
They would clap their hands for joy.

                                    But,
No matter, for in stunning soundlessness, it
Explodes, and over the city a bright mist
Descends of—microscopically—spit.

5
THE JET MUST BE HUNTING FOR SOMETHING

One cop holds the spic delicately between thumb and forefinger.
It is as though he did not want to get a white glove dirty.

The jet prowls the sky and Penn Station looks bombed-out.

The spic has blood over one eye. He had tried to run away.
He will not try again, and in that knowledge, his face is
                                    as calm as congealing bacon grease.

Three construction workers come out from behind the hoarding.

The two cops are not even talking to each other, and in spite of
The disturbance you are so metronomically creating, ignore
                                    you. They are doing their duty.

The jet prowls. I do not know what it is hunting for.

The three construction workers are looking at you like a technical
Problem. I look at them. One looks at his watch. For everything
                                    there is a season.

How long since last I heard birdsong in the flowery hedgerows of France?
    *

Just now, when I looked at you, I had the distinct impression
                    that you were staring me straight in the eye, and
Who wants to be a piece of white paper filed for eternity on
                    the sharp point of a filing spindle?

The orange-colored helmets of the construction workers
                    bloom brilliant as zinnias.

When you were a child in Georgia, a lard-can of zinnias
                    bloomed by the little cabin door.
Your mother had planted them in the lard-can. People
                    call zinnias nigger-flowers.

Nobody wants to be a piece of white paper filed in the dark
                    on the point of a black-enameled spindle forever.

The jet is so far off there is no sound, not even the sizzle
                    it makes as it sears the utmost edges of air.
It prowls the edge of distance like the raw edge of experience.
                    Oh, reality!

I do not know what the jet is hunting for. But it must
                    be hunting for something.

6
BE SOMETHING ELSE

Be something else, be something
        That is not what it is, for
        Being what it is, it is
        Too absolute to be.

If you insist on being
        What you are, how can we

Ever love you, we
Cannot love what is—

By which I mean a thing that
        Totally is and therefore
        Is absolute, for we
        Know that the absolute is

Delusion, and that Truth lives
        Only in relation—oh!
        We love you, we truly
        Do, and we love the

World, but we know
        We cannot love others unless
        We learn how to love
        Ourselves properly, and we truly

Want to love you, but

For God's sake stop that yelling!

        7
THE WORLD IS A PARABLE

I must hurry, I must go somewhere
Where you are not, where you
Will never be, I
Must go somewhere where
Nothing is real, for only
Nothingness is real and is
A sea of light. The world
Is a parable and we are
The meaning. The traffic
Begins to move, and meaning

133

In my guts blooms like
A begonia, I dare not
Pronounce its name.—Oh, driver!
For God's sake catch that light, for

There comes a time for us all when we want to begin a new life.

All mythologies recognize that fact.

8
DRIVER, DRIVER

Driver, driver, hurry now—
Yes, driver, listen now, I
Must change the address, I want to go to

A place where nothing is the same.
My guts are full of chyme and chyle, of Time and bile, my head
Of visions, I do not even know what the pancreas is for, what,

Driver, driver, is it for?
Tell me, driver, tell me true, for
The traffic begins to move, and that fool ambulance at last,

Screaming, screaming, now arrives.
Jack-hammers are trying, trying, they
Are trying to tell me something, they speak in code.

Driver, do you know the code?
Tat-tat-tat—my head is full of
The code, like Truth or a migraine, and those men in orange helmets,

They must know it, they must know,
For *tat-tat*, they make the hammers go, and
So must know the message, know all the slithery functions of
    *

All those fat slick slimy things that
Are so like a tub full of those things you would find
In a vat in the back room of a butcher shop, but wouldn't eat, but

Are not that, for they are you.
Driver, do you truly, truly,
Know what flesh is, and if it is, as some people say, really sacred?

Driver, there's an awful glitter in the air. What is the weather forecast?

III

In the Mountains

SKIERS

To Baudouin and Annie de Moustier

With the motion of angels, out of
Snow-spume and swirl of gold mist, they
Emerge to the positive sun. At
That great height, small on that whiteness,
With the color of birds or of angels,
They swoop, sway, descend, and descending,
Cry their bright bird-cries, pure
In the sweet desolation of distance.
They slowly enlarge to our eyes. Now
On the flat where the whiteness is
Trodden and mud-streaked, not birds now,
Nor angels even, they stand. They

Are awkward, not yet well adjusted
To this world, new and strange, of Time and
Contingency, who now are only
Human. They smile. The human

Face has its own beauty.

FOG

[1]
White, white, luminous but
Blind—fog on the
Mountain, and the mountains

Gone, they are not here,
And the sky gone. My foot
Is set on what I

Do not see. Light rises
From the cold incandescence of snow
Not seen, and the world, in blindness,

Glows. Distance is
Obscenity. All, all
Is here, no other where.

The heart, in this silence, beats.

[2]
Heart—contextless—how
Can you, hung in this
Blank mufflement of white

Brightness, now know
What you are? Fog,
At my knees, coils, my nostrils

Receive the luminous blindness,
And deeper, deeper, it, with the
Cold gleam of fox-fire among

The intricate secrets of
The lungs, enters, an eye

Screams in the belly. The eye

Sees the substance of body dissolving.

[3]

At fog-height, unseen,
A crow calls, the call,
On the hem of silence, is only

A tatter of cold contempt, then
Is gone. Yes, try to remember
An act that once you thought worthy.

The body's brags are put
To sleep—all, all. What
Is the locus of the soul?

What, in such absoluteness,
Can be prayed for? Oh, crow,
Come back, I would hear your voice:

That much, at least, in this whiteness.

from

TALE OF TIME
Poems 1960-1966

TALE OF TIME

I
WHAT HAPPENED

It was October. It was the Depression. Money
Was tight. Hoover was not a bad
Man, and my mother
Died, and God
Kept on, and keeps on,
Trying to tie things together, but

It doesn't always work, and we put the body
Into the ground, dark
Fell soon, but not yet, and
Have you seen the last oak leaf of autumn, high,
Not yet fallen, stung
By last sun to a gold
Painful beyond the pain one can ordinarily
Get? What

Was there in the interim
To do, the time being the time
Between the clod's *chunk* and
The full realization, which commonly comes only after
Midnight? That

Is when you will go to the bathroom for a drink of water.
You wash your face in cold water.
You stare at your face in the mirror, wondering
Why now no tears come, for
You had been proud of your tears, and so
You think of copulation, of
Fluid ejected, of
Water deeper than daylight, of

The sun-dappled dark of deep woods and
Blood on green fern frond, of
The shedding of blood, and you will doubt
The significance of your own experience. Oh,
Desolation—oh, if
You were rich!
You try to think of a new position. Is this

Grief? You pray
To God that this be grief, for
You want to grieve.

This, you reflect, is no doubt the typical syndrome.

But all this will come later.
There will also be the dream of the eating of human flesh.

II
THE MAD DRUGGIST

I come back to try to remember the faces she saw every day.
She saw them on the street, at school, in the stores, at church.
They are not here now, they have been withdrawn, are put away.
They are all gone now, and have left me in the lurch.

I am in the lurch because they were part of her.
Not clearly remembering them, I have therefore lost that much
Of her, and if I do remember,
I remember the lineaments only beyond the ice-blur and soot-smutch

Of boyhood contempt, for I had not thought they were real.
The real began where the last concrete walk gave out
And the smart-weed crawled in the cracks, where the last privy canted
                                                      to spill
Over flat in the rank-nourished burdock, and would soon, no doubt,
        *

If nobody came to prop it, which nobody would do.
The real began there: field and woods, stone and stream began
Their utterance, and the fox, in his earth, knew
Joy; and the hawk, like philosophy, hung without motion, high,
                              where the sun-blaze of wind ran.

Now, far from Kentucky, planes pass in the night, I hear them and all,
                              all is real.
Some men are mad, but I know that delusion may be one name for truth.
The faces I cannot remember lean at my bed-foot, and grin fit to kill,
For we now share a knowledge I did not have in my youth.

There's one I remember, the old druggist they carried away.
They put him in Hoptown, where he kept on making his list—
The same list he had on the street when he stopped my mother to say:
"Here they are, Miss Ruth, the folks that wouldn't be missed,

"Or this God-durn town would be lucky to miss,
If when I fixed a prescription I just happened to pour
Something in by way of improvement." Then leaned in that gray way
                              of his:
"But you—you always say something nice when you come in my store."

In Hoptown he worked on his list, which now could have nothing to do
With the schedule of deaths continuing relentlessly,
To include, in the end, my mother, as well as that list-maker who
Had the wit to see that she was too precious to die:

A fact some in the street had not grasped—nor the attending physician,
                              nor God, nor I.

III
ANSWER YES OR NO

Death is only a technical correction of the market.
Death is only the transfer of energy to a new form.
Death is only the fulfillment of a wish.

Whose wish?

IV
THE INTERIM

1
Between the clod and the midnight
The time was.
There had been the public ritual and there would be
The private realization,
And now the time was, and

In that time the heart cries out for coherence.
Between the beginning and the end, we must learn
The nature of being, in order
In the end to be, so

Our feet, in first dusk, took
Us over the railroad tracks, where
Sole-leather ground drily against cinders, as when
Tears will not come. She

Whom we now sought was old. Was
Sick. Was dying. Was
Black. Was.
Was: and was that enough? Is
Existence the adequate and only target
For the total reverence of the heart?
                *

We would see her who,
Also, had held me in her arms.
She had held me in her arms,
And I had cried out in the wide
Day-blaze of the world. But

Now was a time of endings.

What is love?

2

Tell me what love is, for
The harvest moon, gold, heaved
Over the far woods which were,
On the black land black, and it swagged over
The hill-line. That light
Lay gold on the roofs of Squiggtown, and the niggers
Were under the roofs, and
The room smelled of urine.
A fire burned on the hearth:
Too hot, and there was no ventilation, and

You have not answered my question.

3

Propped in a chair, lying down she
Could not have breathed, dying
Erect, breath
Slow from the hole of the mouth, that black
Aperture in the blackness which
Was her face, but
How few of them are really
Black, but she
Is black, and life
Spinning out, spilling out, from
The holes of the eyes: and the eyes are
Burning mud beneath a sky of nothing.
The eyes bubble like hot mud with the expulsion of vision.
*

I lean, I am the
Nothingness which she
Sees.

Her hand rises in the air.
It rises like revelation.
It moves but has no motion, and
Around it the world flows like a dream of drowning.
The hand touches my cheek.
The voice says: *you.*

I am myself.

The hand has brought me the gift of myself.

4

I am myself, and
Her face is black like cave-blackness, and over
That blackness now hangs death, gray
Like cobweb over the blackness of a cave, but
That blackness which she is, is
Not deficiency like cave-blackness, but is
Substance.
The cobweb shakes with the motion of her breath.

My hand reaches out to part that grayness of cobweb.

My lips touch the cheek, which is black.
I do not know whether the cheek is cold or hot, but I
Know that
The temperature is shocking.
I press my lips firmly against that death,
I try to pray.

The flesh is dry, and tastes of salt.

My father has laid a twenty-dollar bill on the table.
He, too, will kiss that cheek.

5

We stand in the street of Squigg town.
The moon is high now and the tin roofs gleam.
My brother says: *The whole place smelled of urine.*
My father says: *Twenty dollars—oh, God, what*
Is twenty dollars when
The world is the world it is!

The night freight is passing.
The couplings clank in the moonlight, the locomotive
Labors on the grade.
The freight disappears beyond the coal chute westward, and
The red caboose light disappears into the distance of the continent.
It will move all night into distance.

My sister is weeping under the sky.
The sky is enormous in the absoluteness of moonlight.

These are factors to be considered in making any final estimate.

6

There is only one solution. If
You would know how to live, here
Is the solution, and under
My window, when ice breaks, the boulder
Groans in the gorge, the foam swirls, and in
The intensity of the innermost darkness of steel
The crystal blooms like a star, and at
Dawn I have seen the delicate print of the coon-hand in silt by the riffle.

Hawk-shadow sweetly sweeps the grain.
I would compare it with that fugitive thought which I can find no
                                                             word for.

7

Planes pass in the night. I turn
To the right side if the beating
Of my own heart disturbs me.

The sound of water flowing is
An image of Time, and therefore
Truth is all and
Must be respected, and
On the other side of the mirror into which,
At morning, you will stare, History

Gathers, condenses, crouches, breathes, waits. History
Stares forth at you through the eyes which
You think are the reflection of
Your own eyes in the mirror.
Ah, Monsieur du Miroir!

Your whole position must be reconsidered.

8

But the solution: You
Must eat the dead.
You must eat them completely, bone, blood, flesh, gristle, even
Such hair as can be forced. You
Must undertake this in the dark of the moon, but
At your plenilune of anguish.

Immortality is not impossible,
Even joy.

V

WHAT WERE YOU THINKING, DEAR MOTHER?

What were you thinking, a child, when you lay,
At the whippoorwill hour, lost in the long grass,
As sun, beyond the dark cedars, sank?
You went to the house. The lamps were now lit.
                *

What did you think when the evening dove mourned,
Far off in those sober recesses of cedar?
What relevance did your heart find in that sound?
In lamplight, your father's head bent at his book.

What did you think when the last saffron
Of sunset faded beyond the dark cedars,
And on noble blue now the evening star hung?
You found it necessary to go to the house,

And found it necessary to live on,
In your bravery and in your joyous secret,
Into our present maniacal century,
In which you gave me birth, and in

Which I, in the public and private mania,
Have lived, but remember that once I,
A child, in the grass of that same spot, lay,
And the whippoorwill called, beyond the dark cedars.

VI
INSOMNIA

1

If to that place. Place of grass.
If to hour of whippoorwill, I.
If I now, not a child. To.
If now I, not a child, should come to
That place, lie in
That place, in that hour hear
That call, would
I rise,
Go?
*

Yes, enter the darkness. Of.
Darkness of cedars, thinking
You there, you having entered, sly,
My back being turned, face
Averted, or
Eyes shut, for
A man cannot keep his eyes steadily open
Sixty years.

I did not see you when you went away.

Darkness of cedars, yes, entering, but what
Face, what
Bubble on dark stream of Time, white
Glimmer un-mooned? Oh,
What age has the soul, what
Face does it wear, or would
I meet that face that last I saw on the pillow, pale?

I recall each item with remarkable precision.

Would the sweat now be dried on the temples?

    2
What would we talk about? The dead,
Do they know all, or nothing, and
If nothing, does
Curiosity survive the long unravelment? Tell me

What they think about love, for I
Know now at long last that the living remember the dead only
Because we cannot bear the thought that they
Might forget us. Or is
That true? Look, look at these—
But no, no light here penetrates by which
You might see these photographs I keep in my wallet. Anyway,
I shall try to tell you all that has happened to me.

Though how can I tell when I do not even know?
    *

And as for you, and all the interesting things
That must have happened to you and that
I am just dying to hear about—

But would you confide in a balding stranger
The intimate secret of death?

3

Or does the soul have many faces, and would I,
Pacing the cold hypothesis of Time, enter
Those recesses to see, white,
Whiter than moth-wing, the child's face
Glimmer in cedar gloom, and so
Reach out that I might offer
What protection I could, saying,
"I am older than you will ever be"—for you
Are the child who once
Lay lost in the long grass, sun setting.

Reach out, saying: "Your hand—
Give it here, for it's dark and, my dear,
You should never have come in the woods when it's dark,
But I'll take you back home, they're waiting."
And to woods-edge we come, there stand.

I watch you move across the open space.
You move under the paleness of new stars.
You move toward the house, and one instant,

A door opening, I see
Your small form black against the light, and the door
Is closed, and I

Hear night crash down a million stairs.
In the ensuing silence
My breath is difficult.
Heat lightning ranges beyond the horizon.

That, also, is worth mentioning.

4

Come,
Crack crust, striker
From darkness, and let seize—let what
Hand seize, oh!—my heart, and compress
The heart till, after pain, joy from it
Spurt like a grape, and I will grind
Teeth on flint tongue till
The flint screams. Truth
Is all. But

I must learn to speak it
Slowly, in a whisper.

Truth, in the end, can never be spoken aloud,
For the future is always unpredictable.
But so is the past, therefore

At wood's edge I stand, and,
Over the black horizon, heat lightning
Ripples the black sky. After
The lightning, as the eye
Adjusts to the new dark,
The stars are, again, born.

They are born one by one.

HOMAGE TO EMERSON, ON NIGHT FLIGHT TO NEW YORK

To Peter and Ebie Blume

I
HIS SMILE

Over Peoria we lost the sun:
The earth, by snow like sputum smeared, slides
Westward. Those fields in the last light gleam. Emerson—

The essays, on my lap, lie. A finger
Of light, in our pressurized gloom, strikes down,
Like God, to poke the page, the page glows. There is
No sin. Not even error. Night,

On the glass at my right shoulder, hisses
Like sand from a sand-blast, but
The hiss is a sound that only a dog's
Ear could catch, or the human heart. My heart

Is as abstract as an empty
Coca-Cola bottle. It whistles with speed.
It whines in that ammoniac blast caused by
The passage of stars, for
At 38,000 feet Emerson

Is dead right. His smile
Was sweet as he walked in the greenwood.
He walked lightly, his toes out, his body
Swaying in the dappled shade, and
His smile never withered a violet. He
               *

Did not even know the violet's name, not having
Been introduced, but he bowed, smiling,
For he had forgiven God everything, even the violet.

When I was a boy I had a wart on the right forefinger.

II
THE WART

At 38,000 feet you had better
Try to remember something specific, if
You yourself want to be something specific, I remember
The wart and the old colored man, he said, *Son*
You quit that jack-off, and that thing go way,
And I said *Quit what,* and he giggled *He-he,* and he
Said, *You is got white skin and hair red as a ter-mater, but*
You is human-kind, but

At 38,000 feet that is hard to remember.

III
THE SPIDER

The spider has more eyes than I have money.
I used to dream that God was a spider, or

Vice versa, but it is easier
To dream of a funnel, and you
The clear liquid being poured down it, forever.
  *

You do not know what is beyond the little end of the funnel.

The liquid glimmers in darkness, you
Are happy, it pours easily, without fume.

All you have to do is not argue.

IV
ONE DRUNK ALLEGORY

Not argue, unless, that is, you are the kind
That needs to remember something specific
In order to be, at 38,000 feet, whatever you are, and once
In New Orleans, in French Town, in
Front of the Old Absinthe House, and it
Was Saturday night, was 2 A.M., a drunk

Crip slipped, and the air was full of flying crutches
Like a Texas tornado exploding with chicken feathers and
Split boards off busted hen-houses, and bingo!—
It was prize money flat on its you-know-what, it
Was like a box of spilled spaghetti, but
I managed to reassemble everything and prop it

Against a lamp post. *Thank you,*
It said in its expensive Harvard-cum-cotton
Voice, then bingo!—
Flat on its you-know-what, on the pavement,
And ditto the crutches. *Prithee,* the voice

Expensively said, *do not trouble yourself
Further. This is as good a position as any
From which to watch the stars.* Then added:
Until, of course, the cops come. I

Had private reasons for not wanting to be
There when the cops came. So wasn't.

Emerson thought that significance shines through everything,

And at that moment I was drunk enough to think all this was allegory.
If it was, it was sure-God one drunk allegory, and
Somewhere in the womb-gloom of the DC-8

A baby is crying. The cry seems to have a reality
Independent of the baby. The cry
Is like a small white worm in my brain.

It nibbles with tiny, insistent assiduity. Its teeth
Are almost too soft. Sometimes it merely tickles.

To my right, far over Kentucky, the stars are shining.

V
MULTIPLICATION TABLE

If the Christmas tree at Rockefeller Center were
A billion times bigger, and you laid it
Flat down in the dark, and
With a steam roller waist-high to God and heavy as
The Rocky Mountains, flattened it out thin as paper, but
Never broke a single damned colored light bulb, and they were all
Blazing in the dark, that would be the way it is, but

Beyond the lights it is dark, and one night in winter, I
Stood at the end of a pier at Coney Island, while
The empty darkness howled like a dog, but no wind, and far down
The boardwalk what must have been a cop's flashlight
Jiggled fitfully over what must have been locked store-fronts, then,
Of a sudden, went out. The stars were small and white, and I heard
*

The sea secretly sucking the piles of the pier with a sound like
An old woman sucking her teeth in the dark before she sleeps.

The nose of the DC-8 dips, and at this point
The man sitting beside me begins, quite audibly, to recite
The multiplication table.

                    Far below,
Individual lights can be seen throbbing like nerve ends.
I have friends down there, and their lives have strange shapes
Like eggs splattered on the kitchen floor. Their lives shine
Like oil-slicks on dark water. I love them, I think.

In a room, somewhere, a telephone keeps ringing.

VI
WIND

The wind comes off the Sound, smelling
Of ice. It smells
Of fish and burned gasoline. A sheet
Of newspaper drives in the wind across
The great distance of cement that bleeds
Off into blackness beyond the red flares. The air

Shivers, it shakes like Jello with
The roar of jets—yes, why
Is it you think you can hear the infinitesimal scrape
Of that newspaper as it slides over the black cement, forever?

The wind gouges its knuckles into my eye. No wonder there are tears.

VII
DOES THE WILD ROSE?

When you reach home tonight you will see
That the envelope containing the policy
Of your flight insurance is waiting, unopened,
On the table. All had been in order,
In case—but can you tell me,

> *Does the wild rose know your secret*
> *As the summer silence breathes?*

Eastward, the great waters stretch in darkness.
Do you know how gulls sleep when they can't make it home?

> *Tell me, tell me, does the wild rose*—tell me, for

Tonight I shall dream of small white stars
Falling forever in darkness like dandruff, but

Now let us cross that black cement which so resembles the arctic ice of
Our recollections. There is the city, the sky
Glows, glows above it, there must be

A way by which the process of living can become Truth.

Let us move toward the city. Do you think you could tell me
What constitutes the human bond? Do you ever think
Of a face half in shadow, tears—
As it would seem from that muted glitter—in the
Eyes, but

The lips do not tremble.

Is it merely a delusion that they seem about to smile?

SHOES IN RAIN JUNGLE

Shoes rot off feet before feet
Rot, and before feet
Stop moving feet
Rot, rot in the
Rain, moving.

Napoleon was wrong, an army
Marches on its feet. If
It has them. If
The feet have shoes.

The Battle of Gettysburg was fought for shoes.
It is hell to die barefoot, unless,
Of course, that is the way you are raised.

They are cheap, but shoes are dear, and

All wars are righteous. Except when
You lose them. This
Is the lesson of history. This—
And shoes. On rotting shoe leather

Men march into history, and when
You get there take a good look around, lost
In the multitudinous gray portieres of beaded
Rain, and say, "*Mot de Cambronne*, this
Is history."

Now you know what it is.

History is what you can't
Resign from, but

There is always refuge in the practice
Of private virtue,
Or at least in heroism, and if
        *

You get stuck with heroism you can, anyway,
When the cameras pop, cover your face,
Like the man who, coming out of the D. A.'s office,
Lifts his hands, handcuffed, to cover his face.

You can do that much.

Melville, ruined, sick, acerb, anent
The Civil War, said: "Nothing
Can lift the heart of man
Like manhood in a fellow-man," and

Sociologists should make a study called "Relative
Incidence of Mention of Heroes in News Media
As Index to Gravity of a Situation."

Sociologists can do that much.

And when the rainy season is over
There will be new problems, including
The problem of a new definition of virtue.

Meanwhile talk as little *mot de Cambronne* as
Possible, and remember
There is more than one kind of same.

This last is very important.

PATRIOTIC TOUR AND POSTULATE OF JOY

Once, once, in Washington,
D.C., in June,
All night—I swear it—a single mockingbird
Sang,
Sang to the Presidential ear,

Wherein it poured
Such criticism and advice as that ear
Had rarely had the privilege to hear.

And sang to every senator
Available,
And some, as sources best informed affirm,
Rose,
Rose with a taste in the throat like bile,
To the bathroom fled
And spat, and faced the mirror there, and while
The bicarb fizzed, stared, feet cold on tile.

And sang to Edgar Hoover, too,
And as it preached
Subversion and all bright disaster, he
Woke;
Woke, then looked at Mom's photo, so heard
No more. But far,
Far off in Arlington, the heroes stirred
And meditated on the message of that bird.

And sang—oh, merciless!—to me,
Who to that place
And to that massive hour had moved, and now
Rose,
Rose naked, and shivered in moonlight, and cried
Out in my need
To know what postulate of joy men have tried
To live by, in sunlight and moonlight, until they died.

WAYS OF DAY

I have come all this way.
I am sitting in the shade.
Book on knee and mind on nothing,

I now fix my gaze
On my small son playing in the afternoon's blaze.

Convulsive and cantankerous,
Night heaved, and burning, the star
Fell. What do I remember?
I heard the swamp owl, night-long, call.
The far car's headlight swept the room wall.

I am the dark and tricky one.
I am watching from my shade.
Your tousled hair-tips prickle the sunlight.
I watch you at your sunlit play.
Teach me, my son, the ways of day.

FALL COMES IN BACK-COUNTRY VERMONT
To William Meredith

(1   One Voter Out of Sixteen)
Deader they die here, or at least
Differently, deeper the hole, and after
The burying, at night, late, you
Are more apt to wonder about the drainage

Of the cemetery, but know that you needn't, for
Here's all hills anyway, or mountain, and the hole
Standard, but if no drainage problem, yet
You may still wake with a kind of psychic

Twitch, as when the nerves in the amputee's
Stump (a saw did it, no doubt) twitch and wonder
How that which has gone off and set up
As a separate self is making out, and whether
*

It repents of its rashness, and would like
To come back and crawl into bed and be
Forgiven, and even though you, like me,
May forget the name of the dead, in the dark you

Can't help but remember that if there are only
Sixteen voters and one dies, that leaves only
Fifteen, and no doubt you know the story
Of how it began, how he laid his axe down, then

Just sat on a log, not saying a word, till
The crew knocked off for the day, and never
Came back (it was cancer), and later you'd see him
Sit on the porch in the sun and throw bread

To the chipmunks, but that was last year, and now
There's the real-estate sign in the yard, and the grass
Not cut, and already one window knocked out,
For the widow's heartbroken and gone, and the bed

Is stripped to the mattress, and the bedpan
Washed with ammonia and put on a high shelf,
And the stuffed lynx he shot now all night glares
At the empty room with a feral vindication,

And does not forgive, and thinks with glee
How cancer is worse than a 30.30, and

        (2   The Bear and the Last Person to Remember)
It is well the widow is gone, for here winter's
Not made for a woman lone, lorn, and slow-foot,
And summer already sinks southward, and soon
All over the state the summer people

Will put the lawn mower in the red barn, drain
The plumbing, deny the pain of that heart-pinch
They cannot define, and get out the suitcase
To pack, for last night, in moonlight and high
        *

On the mountain, I heard the first bear-hoot,
As the bear that all day had stripped bushes of the last
Blueberries, felt that hot itch and heaved
Up his black, hairy man-height in moonlight,

Lifted the head and curled back the black lip
To show the white moon-gleam of tusk, and the throat
Pulsed in that call that is like the great owl's,
But more edged with anguish, and then far off,

From a ruined orchard, by the old cellar hole,
In the tang and tawny air-taste of the apple-
Night, the she bear, too, rises,
And the half-crushed apple, forgotten, falls

From the jaw gone slack in that moment before
Her utterance, and soon now, night after night,
On the mountain the moon-air will heave with that hunger,
So that, in that hour, the boys of the village

Come out, climb a ridge and reply, and when
Off on the mountain that hoot comes, and nearer,
The girls with them shiver and giggle, not quite
Daring to face that thought that from dark now,

Hot-breathed and hairy, earth-odored and foam-flecked,
Rises, and want to go home, all but one,
Who feels that the night cannot breathe, and who soon,
On the raw mattress, in that house, will cry

Out, but the house is empty, and
Through the window where once the lace curtains hung
And a green shade was but is not,
The moonlight now pours like God, and the sweat

Of her effort goes ice, for she remembers,
So struggles to thrust off that weight that chokes her,
Thrusts herself up on that mattress, and gasping
In that ice and ice-iron of moonlight, with

*

What breath in that dishevelment
Is possible, says: "But here—it was here—
On this bed that he died, and I'll catch it and die"—
But does not, comes back, comes back until snow flies,

And many years later will be the last person
To remember his name who there on that bed

      (3   The Human Fabric)
Had died, but for now let us take some comfort
In the fact that the fifteen surviving voters,
Remembering his name, feel, in the heart,
Diminished, for in this section death

Is a window gone dark and a face not seen
Any more at the P. O., and in the act
Of rending irreparably the human fabric,
Death affirms the fact of that fabric, so what

If at night, in first snow, the hunters pass—
Pale clerks and mechanics from Springfield and Hartford
With red caps and rifles and their pitiful
Blood-lust and histrionic maleness—and passing,

Throw out from the car the empty bourbon
Bottle to lie in the snow by the For-
Sale sign, and snow covers the bottle, will cover
The sign itself, and then the snow plow

Will pile up the banks as high as the eaves,
So that skiers who sing past in sports cars at dusk
Cannot see it, nor singing, need yet to know
The truth which at last they will come to need,

That life is of life paradigm, and death
The legend of death, nor need ever to know

(4   Afterwards)
That all night, eaves-high, the snow will press
Its face to the black ice of glass, and by
The white light its own being sheds, stare
Into that trapped cubicle of emptiness which

Is that room, but by that time I
Will not be here, in another place be,
And in my bed, not asleep, will endeavor
To see in my mind the eagle that once,

Above sunset, above the mountain in Stratton,
I saw—on thinnest air, high, saw
Lounging—oh, look!—it turns, and turning,
Shoulders like spray that last light before

The whistling down-plunge to the mountain's shade.

I touch the hand there on the pillow.

THE DAY DR. KNOX DID IT

To William and Rose Styron

I
PLACE AND TIME

Heat-blaze, white dazzle: and white is the dust
down the only street of Cerulean Springs,
which is only a piece of country road
mislaid, somehow, among the white houses,

as the houses, too, had got mislaid
among the last big oaks and big tulip trees left
from the old forest-time. But to resume:
heat-dazzle, dust-whiteness—an image in sleep,

or in the brain behind the eyeball,
as now, in the light of this other day,
and year, the eyeball, stunned by that inner
blaze, sees nothing, can nothing see

outward whatsoever—only
the white dust of that street, and it
is always August, is 3 P.M.,
the mercury 95, and the leaf

of the oak tree curls at the edge like leather,
and the post master's setter pants in his cave
of cool back under the rotting floor boards
of the P. O.'s high old porch, and every

shade is down in every house,
and the last ash winks in the black kitchen range,
and the iron creaks with contraction in the lonely
new silence of the kitchen. Far off,

*

when the head of the moccasin parts the green
algae and it slides up out of the slough,
its trail on the stone sizzles dry in a twinkling,
and the lunacy of the cicada knows

now no remission. The sun is white.
It fills the sky with a scream of whiteness,
and my feet move in the white dust.
My feet are bare, I am nine years old,

and my feet in the white dust move, but I move
in a dream that is silver like willow and water
and the glimmer of water on water-dark stone.
I see in my mind that place I will go.

This is the summer of 1914.
I move toward that coolness. Then I hear the sound.

II
THE EVENT

The sound was like one made by a board
dropped from a builder's scaffold to fall
flat and heavy on another
board grounded solid and flat to make

the sound solid. But cottony, too,
as though its own echoes were tangled in it,
in thickness and softness—an effect that was caused,
no doubt, by the fact he had climbed to the barn loft

to arrange himself. That summer I'd played
there in that loft, and so knew how
if you lay on your back in the hay, all
you could see was the twilight of spider-web
    *

hung from the rooftree, or maybe one wasp
cruising slow in that gloom with one
sharp glint of light on his hard sheen.
That man—how long had he lain, just looking?

That was the thing that stuck in my head.
I would wonder how long he had lain there, first.

III

A CONFEDERATE VETERAN TRIES TO
EXPLAIN THE EVENT

"But why did he do it, Grandpa?" I said
to the old man sitting under the cedar,
who had come a long way to that place, and that time
when that younger man lay down in the hay

to arrange himself. And now the old man
lifted his head to stare at me.
"It's one of those things," he said, and stopped.
"What things?" I said. And he said: "Son—

"son, one of those things you never know."
"But there must be a *why*," I said. Then he
said: "Folks—yes, folks, they up and die."
"But, Grandpa—" I said. And he: "They die."

Said: "Yes, by God, and I've seen 'em die.
I've seen 'em die and I've seen 'em dead.
I've seen 'em die hot and seen 'em die cold.
Hot lead and cold steel—" The words, they stopped.

The mouth closed up. The eyes looked away.
Beyond the lawn where the fennel throve,

beyond the fence where the whitewash peeled,
beyond the cedars along the lane,

the eyes fixed. The land, in sunlight,
swam, with the meadow the color of rust,
and distance the blue of Time, and nothing—
oh, nothing—would ever happen, and

in the silence my breath did not happen. But
the eyes, they happened, they found me, I
stood there and waited. "Dying," he said,
"hell, dying's a thing any fool can do."

"But what made him do it?" I said, again.
Then wished I hadn't, for he stared at me.
He stared at me as though I weren't there,
or as though I were dead, or had never been born,

and I felt like dandelion fuzz blown away,
or a word you'd once heard but never could spell,
or only an empty hole in the air.
From the cedar shade his eyes burned red.

Darker than shade, his mouth opened then.
Spit was pink on his lips, I saw the tongue move
beyond the old teeth, in the dark of his head.
It moved in that dark. Then, "Son—" the tongue said.

"For some folks the world gets too much," it said.
In that dark, the tongue moved. "For some folks," it said.

IV
THE PLACE WHERE THE BOY POINTED

It was ten days after the event
when the son of the man who had lain in the hay
took me back to the loft where we'd once played,
but this time it wasn't to play, though for what

I didn't know, he just said, "Come on,"
and when I came, and there we stood
in the spider-web gloom and wasp-glint light,
he stood, his face white in shadow, and pointed.

I stared at the place, but the hay was clean,
which was strange, for I'd been hearing them tell
how a 12-gauge will make an awful mess
if you put the muzzle in your mouth.

I kept thinking about how the place looked clean.
I kept wondering who had cleaned up the mess.

V
AND ALL THAT CAME THEREAFTER

But ran from such wondering as I ran
down the street, and the street was dancing a-dazzle,
and the dust rose white in plops round my feet
as they ran toward that stream that was silent and silver

in willow and water, and I would lie
with my eyes shut tight, and let water flow
over me as I lay, and like water, the world
would flow, flow away, on forever. But once
        *

in San Francisco, on Telegraph Hill,
past midnight, alone, and that was
in the time long before that imbecile
tower had there been built, and there I

watched fog swell up from the sea and lean,
and star by star blot the sky out,
and blot the hill, and blot me out
from all relation but to the dry

goat droppings that beneath my feet
pressed the thin soles of my sneakers, as I,
in that swirl of whiteness gone blinder than black,
lifted up my arms, and while distantly

I heard the freighter, savage in fog,
slide past the passage of the Gate,
my own heart, in a rage like joy,
burst. I did not know my name,

nor do I know, even now, the meaning
of another night, by another sea,
when sea-salt on the laurel leaf
in moonlight, like frost, gleamed, and salt

were the tears to my lips on the girl's face, for
she wept, and I did not know why, and thus
entered her body, and in that breathless
instant of poised energy, heard

the sea-sway and the secret grind
of shingle down the glimmering shore.
Later, we lay and heard it. It
from the hollow of earth seemed, but the moon

hung steady as eternity. Now
I sometimes cannot remember her face, nor
the name of the village where we had stayed,
and as for Telegraph Hill, long since
                    *

gone is the immigrant's goat, and there now
wearers of pin-stripe and of furs by I. Magnin
have swarmed in their hives of glass to admire
from that point of vantage the rising values

of real estate and the beauty of stars,
which yet in fact shine, and if there is fog,
high above the last gray unravelment, shine,
while fog-wrapped, the freighters, and troopships now too,

seaward slide, and hooting, proceed
in darkness, and deeper in darkness blooms
the inward orchid, and agon, blind,
of this, our age, of which I—who

have lied, in velleity loved, in weakness
forgiven, who have stolen small objects, committed
adultery, and for a passing pleasure,
as well as for reasons of sanitation,

inflicted death on flies—am,
like you, the perfect image, and if
once through the blaze of that August I fled,
but toward myself I fled, for there is

no water to wash the world away.
We are the world, and it is too late
to pretend we are children at dusk watching fireflies.
We must frame, then, more firmly the idea of good.

My small daughter's dog has been killed on the road.
It is night. In the next room she weeps.

HOLY WRIT

To Vann and Glenn Woodward

I
ELIJAH ON MOUNT CARMEL

(Elijah, after the miraculous fall of fire on his altar, the breaking of the drouth, and the slaughter of the priests of Baal, girds up his loins and runs ahead of the chariot of Ahab to the gates of Jezreel, where Jezebel waits.)

Nothing is re-enacted. Nothing
Is true. Therefore nothing
Must be believed,
But
To have truth
Something must be believed,
And repetition and congruence,
To say the least, are necessary, and
His thorn-scarred heels and toes with filth horn-scaled
Spurned now the flint-edge and with blood spurts flailed
Stone, splashed mud of Jezreel. And he screamed.
He had seen glory more blood-laced than any he had dreamed.

Far, far ahead of the chariot tire,
Which the black mud sucked, he screamed,
Screaming in glory
Like
A bursting blood blister.
Ahead of the mud-faltered fetlock,
He screamed, and of Ahab huddled in
The frail vehicle under the purpling wrack
And spilled gold of storm—poor Ahab, who,
From metaphysical confusion and lightning, had nothing to run to
But the soft Phoenician belly and commercial acuity
Of Jezebel: that darkness wherein History creeps to die.
                *

How could he ever tell her? Get nerve to?
Tell how around her high altar
The prinking and primped
Priests,
Limping, had mewed,
And only the gull-mew was answer,
No fire to heaped meats, only sun-flame,
And the hairy one laughed: "Has your god turned aside to make pee-pee?"
How then on that sea-cliff he prayed, fire fell, sky darkened,
Rain fell, drouth broke now, for God had hearkened,
And priests gave their death-squeal. The king hid his eyes in his coat.
Oh, why to that hairy one should God have hearkened, who smelled
like a goat?

Yes, how could he tell her? When he himself
Now scarcely believed it? Soon,
In the scented chamber,
She,
Saying, "Baby, Baby,
Just hush, now hush, it's all right,"
Would lean, reach out, lay a finger
To his lips to allay his infatuate gabble. So,
Eyes shut, breath scant, he heard her breath rip the lamp-flame
To blackness, and by that sweet dog-bait, lay, and it came,
The soft hand-grope he knew he could not, nor wished to, resist
Much longer; so prayed: "Dear God, dear God—oh, please, don't exist!"

II
SAUL AT GILBOA
(Samuel Speaks)

1
From landscape the color of lions.
From land of great stone the color,
At noon-blaze, of the droppings of lions,

But harder than iron and,
By moonlight, bone-white, and the crouched stone seizes,
In its teeth, the night-wind, and the wind
Yelps, the wind
Yowls. From
The district of dry thorn, the ankle
Scarred by thorn. From
The dry watercourses.
Came.

He had been seeking his father's lost asses.

Sought what he found not, but found
Me, for what
We seek we never
Find, find only fate. Which is,
Not the leaf, but the shadow
Of the leaf, turning in air.

Fate is the air we breathe.

He moved toward me, and in that motion
His body clove the bright air.

2

How beautiful are the young, walking
On the fore-part of the foot, the hair of the head,
Without ointment, glistens, the lower
Lip, though the fat of burnt meat has long since
Been wiped, glistens, and
Eyes with the glister of vision like
The eyes, hunger-whetted, of the eagle
That from the high sky stares.

His hands, by his sides, heavy hang down like hammers.

(Let Amalek shiver in his tent of goat hair.
Let him put belly to belly and no cloth between, not waiting

For the hour when stars, in blackness, are burnished by
The cold wind.)

Toward me he walks, I am old.
Dust of desert on him, and thorn-scar, he
Walks, and is the man. He is,
From the shoulder and upward, higher than any among the people.

He comes walking who will make Israel
One among the nations. He walks
In his youth, which is the sweet affront
Of ignorance, toward me, and I
Smile, feeling my face, even in that smile, go stiff as
Fresh goat hide, unflayed, set in sun, goes,
For the people murmur, say
I am old. A king
They would have, and toward me
He walks who will make all things
New. In beauty toward
My knowledge, walks. What
Is in my heart?

I hear my own voice. It says: *My son.*

    3
Before the knowledge in me, he, beautiful, down in the dirt, kneels.
Desert-travel and dry sweat: his odor
Is like old curds and new wine, and it comes to my nostrils.
His head is bowed, and I see the twin plaitings of muscle
At the back of his neck, and how they are grappled,
Olive root in rock, in shoulder-flesh. They grapple
To great bone, new sweat now
Beads in the channel of the back of his neck below
The skull, the skull is a tower of brass
Bent before me. He
Is ignorant, and I pour
Oil on those locks that no new shining need.
    *

The far hills, white light on gypsum, dazzle.
The hills waver like salt dissolving in water. Swim
In the dazzle of my eyes.

4

I am the past time, am old, but
Am, too, the time to come, for I,
In my knowledge, close my eyes, and am
The membrane between the past and the future, am thin, and
That thinness is the present time, the membrane
Is only my anguish, through which
The past seeps, penetrates, is absorbed into
The future, through which
The future bleeds into, becomes, the past even before
It ceases to be
The future. Am also

The knife edge that divides.

I say to him that the asses of his father that were lost
Are found.

Say to him that at Tabor at
A high place a band of the prophets,
With psaltery and tabret, dancing, will come,
And into him will enter that breath which
Will make him dance.
He will be another man.

Before me, his head is bowed. The oil glistens.

Say he will dance, but I do not say
That that dance is a dance into self-hood—and oh!
Beautiful is ignorance kneeling—and do not
Say how black, when the dance-breath goes out, will be
The blackness, nor say how the young boy
Before him will sit, and strike the harp,
Nor how he at him, because he is young

And the brow smooth, will hurl
The great spear, and the boy will, like smoke, sway,
Slip from his presence, be gone, his foot
Leaving no print among rocks.

He himself will become a friend to darkness, be counseled by wolves.

5

I do not say that I will anoint against him that boy
Of the smooth brow.

Nor say how, at the hour
When the hosts are gathered, he will,
To Endor, in a mantle not his own,
In dark, come. Enter,
And to the woman of the cave speak, for, in the end,
To know is, always, all. To know
Is, whatever the knowledge, the secret hope within
Hope. So to the cave.

And from death, I,
In shape of shadow, rise,
Stand. He bows down
Before me, and in the fierceness of last joy, I see
That the hair of his bent head is
Now streaked with gray, so say
That the breath of the dance which has passed from him will not
Return. In the dirt,

He falls down.

6

The woman, who had cried out, "O thou
Art Saul!" and whose life he held in his hand—
She lifts him, gives him to eat.
She feeds him, morsel
By morsel, he like a child.

His jaws move in the labor of grinding by which life is, but
His eyes are in the distance of
Knowledge. He goes

From the cave. But not before
He has cast down the ring, massy of gold, beside her
Who now lies stretched out, eyes closed, face pressed to earth.

She has not stirred. In the silence my voice says:
"Take it, for it
Is of a man who was once a
King." The clink
Of armor, on stone, muted,
From distance and dark outside, comes,
Ceases. "A king," my voice says, "but
Now goes to be

Himself."

7

I had once poured oil on his head.

It had been in sun-blaze, at
The hour of minimal shadow,
And what shadow fell, fell
Black on stone that swam
White with light.

The cicada was hushed.

He kissed the backs of my hands, rose,
Stood, and was ashamed
Before me, who needs must look upward to his face,
Of his tallness.

The toes of his inordinate sandals
Turned inward somewhat, like
A boy. Of the left foot,
Of the great toe, the nail

Was blackened. Bruised,
In the desert, by stone.

I saw it.

He moved from me in the white light.
The black dwindle in distance which now he
Was, was upheld by
White light as by
A hand. He moved across distance, as across
The broad hand of my knowing.
The palm of my hand was as
Wide as the world and the
Blaze of distance. The fingers
Of my hand itched.

How beautiful are the young, walking!

I closed my eyes. I shuddered in a rage of joy.

      8

The south shoulder of the pass:
And first light, gray, on the right hand,
Came. Not light. Grayness
Not strong enough to cast shadow.

Before redness sudden on east rim, before
The sudden awareness of shadows individual
From eastward, cast by
The random of hunched stones, a stallion,
Far off, neighed, once. I see,
In the shadow of imagination, the beast, dim, large,
Gray as stone. That host
From the shadowy inwardness of which,
Then, a brazen *blat* from horn-throat came,
Lower lay, and westwards.

Gilboa is, of that place, the name. There,
With his son whom the sly harpist had loved

With a love surpassing the love of women,
He died. The great torso, a stake
Thrust upward to twist the gut-tangle, towered
Above the wall of Beth-shan, but
With no authority, ha! For the head

Lies at Gilboa. The sky
Is above it, and
The ant has entered
The eye-arch.

9

The death I have entered is a death
In which I cannot lie down.

I have forgotten, literally, God, and through
The enormous hollow of my head, History
Whistles like a wind.

How beautiful are the young, walking!

If I could weep.

DELIGHT

I
INTO BROAD DAYLIGHT

Out of silence walks delight.
   Delight comes on soundless foot
Into the silence of night,
Or into broad daylight.

Delight comes like surprise.
   Delight will prepare you never.
Delight waits beyond range of your eyes
Till the moment of surprise.

Delight knows its own reason,
   A reason you will never know.
Your will, nor hand, can never seize on
Delight. Delight knows its season.

I have met delight at dawn-crest.
   I have met delight at dove-fall
When sunset reddens the dove's breast.
I may not divulge the rest:

Nor can it be guessed.

II
LOVE: TWO VIGNETTES

1. MEDITERRANEAN BEACH, DAY AFTER STORM

How instant joy, how clang
And whang the sun, how
Whoop the sea, and oh,
Sun, sing, as whiter than
Rage of snow, let sea the spume
Fling.

Let sea the spume, white, fling,
White on blue wild
With wind, let sun
Sing, while the world
Scuds, clouds boom and belly,
Creak like sails, whiter than,
Brighter than,
Spume in sun-song, oho!
The wind is bright.

Wind the heart winds
In constant coil, turning
In the—forever—light.

Give me your hand.

2. DECIDUOUS SPRING

Now, now, the world
All gabbles joy like geese, for
An idiot glory the sky
Bangs. Look!
All leaves are new, are
Now, are
Bangles dangling and
Spangling, in sudden air
Wangling, then
Hanging quiet, bright.
      *

The world comes back, and again
Is gabbling, and yes,
Remarkably worse, for
The world is a whirl of
Green mirrors gone wild with
Deceit, and the world
Whirls green on a string, then
The leaves go quiet, wink
From their own shade, secretly.

Keep still, just a moment, leaves.

There is something I am trying to remember.

III
SOMETHING IS GOING TO HAPPEN

Something is going to happen, I tell you I know.
This morning, I tell you, I saw ice in the bucket.
Something is going to happen and you can't duck it.
The way the wind blows is the way the dead leaves go.
Something is going to happen, and I'm telling you so.

Something is going to happen, I declare it.
It always happens on days like this, Mother said.
No, I didn't make the world, or make apples red,
But if you're a man you'll buck up and try to bear it.
For this morning the sun rose in the east, I swear it.

Something is going to happen, I swear it will.
Men have wept watching water flow,
And feet move fastest down the old track they know.
Look, look!—how light is lying across that hill!
Something may happen today if you don't sit still.
        *

Something is going to happen without a doubt.
If you aren't careful it may happen this very minute.
Have you ever looked in a drawer and found nothing in it?
Have you ever opened your mouth and tried to shout,
But something happened and the shout would not come out?

Something is going to happen whatever you say.
Whether you look out the window or walk in the door
Some things will be less, and other things more.
It's simply no use to turn your head away.
Something is bound to happen on a day like today

To change everything any-which-a-way,
For the sound of your name is only a mouthful of air
And the lost and the found may be found or lost anywhere.
Therefore to prepare you there's one more thing I must say:
Delight may dawn, as the day dawned, calmly, today.

IV
TWO POEMS ABOUT SUDDENLY AND A ROSE

1. DAWN

Suddenly. Is. Now not what was *not*,
But what is. From nothing of *not*
Now all of *is*. All is. Is light, and suddenly
Dawn—and the world, in blaze of *is*,
Burns. Is flame, of time and tense
The bold combustion, and
The flame of *is*, in fury
And ungainsayable updraft of that
Black chimney of what is *not*,
Roars. Christmas—

Remember, remember!—and into flame
All those gay wrappings the children fling, then

In hands of *now*, they hold
Presents of *is*, and while
Flame leaps, they, in joy,
Scream. Oh, children,

Now to me sing, I see
Forever on the leaf the light. Snow
On the pine-leaf, against the bright blue
Forever of my mind, like breath,
Balances. But light,

Is always light, and suddenly,
On any morning, is, and somewhere,
In a garden you will never
See, dew, in fracture of light
And lunacy of gleam-glory, glitters on
A petal red as blood, and

The rose dies, laughing.

2 . INTUITION

Suddenly, suddenly, everything
Happens, it seems. For example, it
Rains—or it does not rain—and suddenly
Life takes on a new dimension, and old pain
Is wisdom—Christ, believe that
And you'll believe anything. But
Everything, some day, is suddenly, and life
Is what you are living, not
What you thought you had lived
All your life, but suddenly
Know you had not—oh, suddenly is what
Mother did not tell, for
How could she when
Suddenly is too sudden to tell, and

The rose dies laughing, suddenly.

V
NOT TO BE TRUSTED

Delight is not to be trusted.
It will betray you.
Delight will undo the work of your hand
In a secret way. You

Cannot trust delight.
As I have told you,
It undoes the ambition of the young and
The wisdom of the old. You

Are not exempt. Though it yet
Has never undone you,
Look! In that bush, with wolf-fang white, delight
Humps now for someone: *You.*

from

YOU, EMPERORS, AND OTHERS

Poems 1957-1960

To Max and Carol Shulman

GARLAND FOR YOU

I
CLEARLY ABOUT YOU

Bene fac, hoc tecum feres.
—ON TOMB OF ROMAN CITIZEN OF NO
HISTORICAL IMPORTANCE, UNDER THE EMPIRE

Whoever you are, this poem is clearly about you,
For there's nothing else in the world it could be about.
Whatever it says, this poem is clearly true,
For truth is all we are born to, and the truth's out.

You won't look in the mirror? Well—but your face is there
Like a face drowned deep under water, mouth askew,
And the tongue in that mouth tastes cold water, not sweet air,
And if it could scream in that medium, the scream would be you.

Your mother preferred the more baroque positions.
Your father's legerdemain marks the vestry accounts.
So you didn't know? Well, it's time you did—though one shuns
To acknowledge the root from which one's own virtue mounts.

In the age of denture and reduced alcoholic intake,
When the crow's dawn-calling stirs memories you'd better eschew,
You will try the cross, or the couch, for balm for the heart's ache—
But that stranger who's staring so strangely, he knows you are you.

Things are getting somewhat out of hand now—light fails on the salt-flat.
In the back lot the soft-faced delinquents are whistling like snipe.
*That letter—why doesn't it come!—*you finger your heart that,
At a touch, in the bosom now bleeds, like a plum over-ripe.
                    *

Burn this poem, though it wring its small hands and try to jerk back.
But no use, for in bed, into your pajama pocket,
It will creep, and sleep as snug as a field mouse in haystack,
And its heart to your heart all night makes a feather-soft racket.

II
THE LETTER ABOUT MONEY, LOVE,
OR OTHER COMFORT, IF ANY

In the beginning was the Word.
—THE GOSPEL ACCORDING TO ST. JOHN

Having accepted the trust so many years back,
 before seven wars, nine coups d'état, and the deaths of friends and
                 friendships,
 before having entered the world of lurkers, shirkers, burkers, tipsters
                and tips,
 or even discovered I had small knack
 for honesty, but only a passion, like a disease, for Truth,
 having, as I have said, accepted the trust
 those long years back in my youth,
 it's no wonder that now I admit, as I must,
 to no recollection whatever
 of wens, moles, scars, or his marks of identification—but do recall my
                disgust
 at the odor of garlic and a somewhat perfervid eye-gleam beneath
            the dark hat of the giver,

Who, as I came up the walk in summer moonlight
 and set foot to the porch step, rose with a cough from beside the
              hydrangea,
 and thrust the thing out at me, as though it were common for any total
              stranger
 to squat by one's door with a letter at night,
 at which, in surprise, I had stopped to stare (the address even then but
             a smudge)

until at the burst of his laugh, like a mirthful catarrh,
I turned, but before I could budge
saw the pattering *V*'s of his shoe tips mar
the moon-snowy dew of the yard,
and be gone—an immigrant type of pointed toe and sleazy insouciance
                            more natural by far
to some Mediterranean alley or merd-spangled *banlieue* than to any
                                  boulevard,

Or surely to Dadston, Tenn., and so I was stuck,
   for though my first thought was to drop the thing in the mail and
                                  forget the affair,
   on second glance I saw what at first I had missed, as though the words
                                hadn't been there:
By Hand Only, and I was dumb-cluck
   enough to drive over to Nashville next day to find the address, but found
   you had blown, the rent in arrears, your bathroom a sty,
   and thus the metaphysical runaround
   which my life became, and for which I
   have mortgaged all, began,
   and I have found milk rotting in bottles inside the back door,
                             and newspapers knee-high
   the carrier had left and never got paid for, and once at my question
                                a child up and ran

Screaming like bloody murder to fall out of breath,
   and once in Dubuque you had sold real estate, and left with a church
                                    letter,
   Episcopal, High, and at the delicious New England farmhouse
                              your Llewellin setter
   was found in the woodshed, starved to death,
   and in Via Margutta you made the attempt, but someone smelled gas
                                  at the door
   in the nick of time, and you fooled with the female Fulbrights
   at the Deux Magots and the Flore,
   until the police caught you dead to rights—
   oh, it's all so human and sad,
   for money and love are terrible things with which to fill
                            all our human days and nights,
   and nobody blames you much, not even I, despite all the trouble I've had,

    *

And still have, on your account, and if it were not
    for encroaching age, new illness, and recurring effects of the beating
    I took from those hoods in the bar in Frisco for the mere fact of merely
                                             repeating

    that financial gossip, and from which I got
    this bum gam, my defect in memory, and a slight stutter—
    but as I was saying, were it not for my infirm years,
    I would try to deliver the letter,
    especially since I was moved nigh to tears
    myself by the tale you'd been caught
    crouching in the dark in the canna bed that pretties the lawn
                              of the orphanage where it appears
    you were raised—yes, crooning among the ruined lilies to a teddy bear,
                                   not what a grown man ought

To be doing past midnight—but be that as it may,
    there's little choice for my future course, given present circumstances,
    and my conscience is clear, for I assure you I've not made a penny,
                                  at least not expenses,
    and so, on the basis of peasant hearsay
    at the goatherd's below timber line, I will go up, and beyond the
                                north face,
    find that shelf where a last glacial kettle, beck, or cirque glints
    blue steel to steel sky in that moon-place,
    and there, while hands bleed and breath stints,
    will, on a flat boulder not
    far from the spot where you at night drink, leave the letter,
                          and my obligation to all intents,
    weighted by stones like a cairn, with a red bandanna to catch your eye,
                                     but what

Good any word of money or love or more casual
    comfort may do now, God only knows, for one who by dog and gun
    has been hunted to the upper altitudes, for the time comes when all
                              men will shun
    you, and you, like an animal,
    will crouch among the black boulders under the knife-edge of
                                night-blast,
    waiting for hunger to drive you down to forage
    for bark, berries, mast,

roots, rodents, grubs, and such garbage,
or a sheep like the one you with your teeth killed,
for you are said to be capable now of all bestiality, and only your age
makes you less dangerous; so, though I've never seen your face and
have fulfilled

The trust, discretion, as well as perhaps a strange shame,
overcomes curiosity, and from that high rubble of the world's wrack,
will send me down to the darkness of trees until, having lost all track,
I stand, bewildered, breath-bated and lame,
at the edge of a clearing, to hear, as first birds stir, life lift now night's
hasp,

then see, in first dawn's drench and drama, the snow peak go gory,
and the eagle will unlatch his crag-clasp,
fall, and at breaking of wing-furl, bark glory,
and by that new light I shall seek
the way, and my peace with God, and if in some taproom travelers pry
into this story,
I shall not reduce it to a drunken marvel, assuming I know the tongue
they speak.

III
MAN IN THE STREET

> Raise the stone, and there thou shalt find Me,
> cleave the wood, there am I.
> —THE SAYINGS OF JESUS

"Why are your eyes as big as saucers—big as saucers?"
I said to the man in the gray flannel suit.
And he said: "I see facts I can't refute—
Winners and losers,
Pickers and choosers,
Takers, refusers,
Users, abusers,
And my poor head, it spins like a top.
It spins and spins, and will not stop."

Thus said the young man I happened to meet,
Wearing his nice new Ivy League flannel suit down the sunlit street.

"What makes you shake like wind in the willows—wind in the willows?"
I said to the man in the black knit tie.
And he said: "I see things before my eye—
Jolly good fellows,
Glad-handers of hellos,
Fat windbags and bellows,
Plumpers of pillows,
And God's sweet air is like dust on my tongue,
And a man can't stand such things very long."
Thus said the young man I happened to meet,
Wearing his gray flannel suit and black knit tie down the sunlit street.

"What makes your face flour-white as a miller's—white as a miller's?"
I said to the man in the Brooks Brothers shirt.
And he said: "I see things that can't help but hurt—
Backers and fillers,
Pickers and stealers,
Healers and killers,
Ticklers and feelers,
And I go to prepare a place for you,
For this location will never do."
Thus said the young man I happened to meet,
Wearing gray flannel suit, knit tie, and Brooks Brothers shirt down the
                                                                    sunlit street.

IV
SWITZERLAND

> . . . *world-mecca for seekers of pleasure and health* . . .
> —TRAVEL AGENCY BROCHURE

After lunch take the half-destroyed bodies and put them to bed.
For a time a mind's active behind the green gloom of the jalousie,

But soon each retires inside the appropriate head
To fondle, like childhood's stuffed bear, some favorite fallacy.

In their pairings the young, of course, have long since withdrawn,
But they take more time to come to the point of siesta:
There's the beach-fatigue and the first digestion to wait on,
So it's three by the time one's adjusted one's darling, and pressed her.

Here's many an old, old friend you have known from long back,
Though of course under different names and with different faces.
Yes, they are the kind of whom you never lose track,
And there's little difference, one finds, between different places.

That's why travel is broadening—you can, for example, expect
The aging alcoholic you once knew in San Diego.
Or the lady theologian who in bed likes best her own intellect:
Lady Hulda House, *Cantab.*—for therapy now trying a dago.

There's the sweet young divorcée whose teacher once said she should
write.
There's the athlete who stares at himself in the glass, by the hour.
There's the old man who can't forgive, and wakes in the night:
Forgive—forgive what? To remember is beyond his power.

And the others and all, they all here re-enact
The acts you'd so shrewdly remarked at the very start,
When in other resorts you first met them—many, in fact,
In that high, highly advertised Switzerland of your own heart.

O God of the *steinbock's* great sun-leap—Thou spike in ice-chasm—
Let down Thy strong hand to all whom their fevers destroy,
And past all their pain, need, greed, lip-biting, and spasm,
Deliver them all, young and old, to Thy health, named joy.

V
ARROGANT LAW

Have you crouched with your rifle, in woods, in autumn,
In earshot of water where at dawn deer come,
Through gold leafage drifting, through dawn-mist like mist,
And the blue steel sweats cold in your fist?
Have you stood on the gunwale in the blaze of sky,
Then with sun blazing black in your inner eye,
Plunged—plunged to break the anchor's deep hold
On rock, where the undercurrents thrill cold?
  Time unwinds like a falling spool.

Have you lain by your love, at night, by willows,
And heard the stream stumble, moon-drunk, at its shallows,
And heard the cows stir, sigh, and shift space,
Then seen how moonlight lay on the girl's face,
With her eyes hieratically closed, and your heart bulged
With what abrupt Truth to be divulged—
But desolate, desolate, turned from your love,
Knowing you'd never know what she then thought of?
  Time unwinds like a falling spool.

Have you stood beside your father's bed
While life retired from the knowledgeable head
To hole in some colding last lurking-place,
And standing there studied that strange face,
Which had endured thunder and even the tears
Of mercy in its human years,
But now, past such accident, seemed to withdraw
Into a more arrogant dispensation, and law?
  Time unwinds like a falling spool.

TWO PIECES AFTER SUETONIUS

I

APOLOGY FOR DOMITIAN

He was not bad, as emperors go, not really—
Not like Tiberius cruel, or poor Nero silly.
The trouble was only that omens said he would die,
So what could he, mortal, do? Not worse, however, than you might, or I.

Suppose from long back you had known the very hour—
"Fear the fifth hour"—and yet for all your power
Couldn't strike it out from the day, or the day from the year,
Then wouldn't you have to strike something at least? If you did,
                                        would it seem so queer?

Suppose you were proud of your beauty, but baldness set in?
Suppose your good leg were dwindling to spindly and thin?
Wouldn't you, like Domitian, try the classic bed-stunt
To prove immortality on what was propped to bear the imperial brunt?

Suppose you had dreamed a gold hump sprouted out of your back,
And such a prosperous burden oppressed you to breath-lack;
Suppose lightning scorched the sheets in your own bedroom;
And from your own statue a storm yanked the name plate and chucked it
                                        into a tomb—

Well, it happened to him. Therefore, there's little surprise
That for hours he'd lock himself up to pull wings from flies.
Fly or man, what odds? He would wander his hall of moonstone,
Mirror-bright so he needn't look over his shoulder to see if he was alone.

Let's stop horsing around—it's not Domitian, it's you
We mean, and the omens are bad, very bad, and it's true

That virtue comes hard vis-à-vis the assiduous clock,
And music, at sunset, faint as a dream, is heard from beyond the burdock,

And as for Domitian, the first wound finds the groin,
And he claws like a cat, but the blade continues to go in,
And the body is huddled forth meanly, and what ritual
It gets is at night, and from his old nurse, a woman poor, nonpolitical.

II
TIBERIUS ON CAPRI

1

All is nothing, nothing all:
To tired Tiberius soft sang the sea thus,
Under his cliff-palace wall.
The sea, in soft approach and repulse,
Sings thus, and Tiberius,
Sea-sad, stares past the dusking sea-pulse
Yonder, where come,
One now by one, the lights, far off, of Surrentum.
He stares in the blue dusk-fall,
For all is nothing, nothing all.

Let darkness up from Asia tower.
On that darkening island behind him *spintriae* now stir.
In grot and scented bower,
They titter, yawn, paint lip, grease thigh,
And debate what role each would prefer
When they project for the Emperor's eye
Their expertise
Of his Eastern lusts and complex Egyptian fantasies.
But darkward he stares in that hour,
Blank now in totality of power.

2

There once, on that goat island, I,
As dark fell, stood and stared where Europe stank.
Many were soon to die—
From acedia snatched, from depravity, virtue,
Or frolic, not knowing the reason, in rank
On rank hurled, or in bed, or in church, or
Dishing up supper,
Or in a dark doorway, loosening the girl's elastic to tup her,
While high in the night sky,
The murderous tear dropped from God's eye;

And faintly forefeeling, forefearing, all
That to fulfill our time, and heart, would come,
I stood on the crumbling wall
Of that foul place, and my lungs drew in
Scent of dry gorse on the night air of autumn,
And I seized, in dark, a small stone from that ruin,
And I made outcry
At the paradox of powers that would grind us like grain, small and dry.
Dark down, the stone, in its fall,
Found the sea: I could do that much, after all.

MORTMAIN

I

AFTER NIGHT FLIGHT SON REACHES BEDSIDE OF ALREADY UNCONSCIOUS FATHER, WHOSE RIGHT HAND LIFTS IN A SPASMODIC GESTURE, AS THOUGH TRYING TO MAKE CONTACT: 1955

In Time's concatenation and
Carnal conventicle, I,
Arriving, being flung through dark and
The abstract flight-grid of sky,
Saw rising from the sweated sheet and
Ruck of bedclothes ritualistically
Reordered by the paid hand
Of mercy—saw rising the hand—

Christ, start again! What was it I,
Standing there, travel-shaken, saw
Rising? What could it be that I,
Caught sudden in gut- or conscience-gnaw,
Saw rising out of the past, which I
Saw now as twisted bedclothes? Like law,
The hand rose cold from History
To claw at a star in the black sky,

But could not reach that far—oh, cannot!
And the star horribly burned, burns,
For in darkness the wax-white clutch could not
Reach it, and white hand on wrist-stem turns,
Lifts in last tension of tendon, but cannot
Make contact—*oh, oop-si-daisy*, churns
The sad heart, *oh, atta-boy, daddio's got*
One more shot in the locker, peas-porridge hot—
       *

But no. Like an eyelid the hand sank, strove
Downward, and in that darkening roar,
All things—all joy and the hope that strove,
The failed exam, the admired endeavor,
Prizes and prinkings, and the truth that strove,
And back of the Capitol, boyhood's first whore—
Were snatched from me, and I could not move,
Naked in that black blast of his love.

II

A DEAD LANGUAGE: CIRCA 1885

Father dead, land lost, stepmother haggard with kids,
Big Brother skedaddling off to Mexico
To make his fortune, gold or cattle or cards,
What could he do but what we see him doing?
Cutting crossties for the first railroad in the region,
Sixteen and strong as a man—was a man, by God!—
And the double-bit bit into red oak, and in that rhythm,
In his head, all day, marched the Greek paradigm:
That was all that was his, and all he could carry all day with him.

Λέγω, λέγεις, λέγει, and the axe swung.
That was that year, and the next year we see him
Revolve in his dream between the piece goods and cheese,
In a crossroads store, between peppermint candy and plow-points,
While the eaves drip, and beyond the black trees of winter
Last light grays out, and in the ruts of the lane
Water gleams, sober as steel. That was that land,
And that was the life, and he reached out and
Took the dime from the gray-scaled palm of the Negro plowhand's hand.

'Εν ἀρχῇ ἦν ὁ λόγος: in the beginning
Was the word, but in the end was
What? At the mirror, lather on chin, with a razor

Big as a corn-knife, or so to the boy it seemed,
He stood, and said: 'Εν ἀρχῇ ἦν ὁ λόγος:
And laughed. And said: "That's Greek, now you know how it sounds!"
And laughed, and waved the bright blade like a toy.
And laughing from the deep of a dark conquest and joy,
Said: "Greek—but it wasn't for me. Let's get to breakfast, boy."

III
FOX-FIRE: 1956

Years later, I find the old grammar, yellowed. Night
Is falling. Ash flakes from the log. The log
Glows, winks, wanes. Westward, the sky,
In one small area redeemed from gray, bleeds dully.
Beyond my window, athwart that red west,
The spruce bough, though snow-burdened, looks black,
Not white. The world lives by the trick of the eye, the trick
Of the heart. I hold the book in my hand, but God
—In what mercy, if mercy?—will not let me weep. But I
Do not want to weep. I want to understand.

Oh, let me understand what is that sound,
Like wind, that fills the enormous dark of my head.
Beyond my head there is no wind, the room
Darkening, the world beyond the room darkening,
And no wind beyond to cleave, unclot, the thickening
Darkness. There must be a way to state the problem.
The statement of a problem, no doubt, determines solution.
If once, clear and distinct, I could state it, then God
Could no longer fall back on His old alibi of ignorance.
I hear now my small son laugh from a farther room.

I know he sits and laughs among his toys,
Teddy bear, letter blocks, yellow dump-truck, derrick, choo-choo—
Bright images, all, of Life's significance.

So I put the book on the shelf, beside my own grammar,
Unopened these thirty years, and leave the dark room,
And know that all night, while the constellations grind,
Beings with folded wings brood above that shelf,
Awe-struck and imbecile, and in the dark,
Amid History's vice and vacuity, that poor book burns
Like fox-fire in the black swamp of the world's error.

IV

IN THE TURPITUDE OF TIME: N.D.

In the turpitude of Time,
Hope dances on the razor edge.
I see those ever-healing feet
Tread the honed edge above despair.
I see the song-wet lip and tossing hair.

The leaf unfolds the autumn weather.
The heart spills the horizon's light.
In the woods, the hunter, weeping, kneels,
And the dappled fawn weeps in contrition
For its own beauty. I hear the toad's intercession

For us, and all, who do not know
How cause flows backward from effect
To bless the past occasion, and
How Time's tongue lifts only to tell,
Minute by minute, what truth the brave heart would fulfill.

Can we—oh, could we only—know
What annelid and osprey know,
And the stone, night-long, groans to divulge?
If only we could, then that star
That dawnward slants might sing to our human ear,
                *

And joy, in daylight, run like feet,
And strength, in darkness, wait like hands,
And between the stone and the wind's voice
A silence wait to become our song:
In the heart's last kingdom only the old are young.

V

A VISION: CIRCA 1880

Out of the woods where pollen is a powder of gold
Shaken from pistil of oak minutely, and of maple,
And is falling, and the tulip tree lifts, not yet tarnished,
The last calyx, in whose chartreuse coolness recessed, dew,
Only this morning, lingered till noon—look,
Out of the woods, barefoot, the boy comes. He stands,
Hieratic, complete, in patched britches and that idleness of boyhood
Which asks nothing and is its own fulfillment:
In his hand a wand of peeled willow, boy-idle and aimless.

Poised between woods and the pasture, sun-green and green shadow,
Hair sweat-dark, brow bearing a smudge of gold pollen, lips
Parted in some near-smile of boyhood bemusement,
Dangling the willow, he stands, and I—I stare
Down the tube and darkening corridor of Time
That breaks, like tears, upon that sunlit space,
And staring, I know who he is, and would cry out.
Out of my knowledge, I would cry out and say:
Listen! Say: *Listen! I know—oh, I know—let me tell you!*

That scene is in Trigg County, and I see it.
Trigg County is in Kentucky, and I have been there,
But never remember the spring there. I remember
A land of cedar-shade, blue, and the purl of limewater,
But the pasture parched, and the voice of the lost joree
Unrelenting as conscience, and sick, and the afternoon throbs,

And the sun's hot eye on the dry leaf shrivels the aphid,
And the sun's heel does violence in the corn-balk.
That is what I remember, and so the scene

I had seen just now in the mind's eye, vernal,
Is altered, and I strive to cry across the dry pasture,
But cannot, nor move, for my feet, like dry corn-roots, cleave
Into the hard earth, and my tongue makes only the dry,
Slight sound of wind on the autumn corn-blade. The boy,
With imperial calm, crosses a space, rejoins
The shadow of woods, but pauses, turns, grins once,
And is gone. And one high oak leaf stirs gray, and the air,
Stirring, freshens to the far favor of rain.

SOME QUIET, PLAIN POEMS

I
ORNITHOLOGY IN A WORLD OF FLUX

It was only a bird call at evening, unidentified,
As I came from the spring with water, across the rocky back-pasture;
But I stood so still sky above was not stiller than sky in pail-water.

Years pass, all places and faces fade, some people have died,
And I stand in a far land, the evening still, and am at last sure
That I miss more that stillness at bird-call than some things that were
                                                            to fail later.

II
HOLLY AND HICKORY

Rain, all night, taps the holly.
It ticks like a telegraph on the pane.
If awake in that house, meditating some old folly
Or trying to live an old pleasure again,
I could hear it sluicing the ruts in the lane.

Rain beats down the last leaf of hickory,
But where I lie now rain-sounds hint less
At benign sleight of the seasons, or Time's adept trickery,
And with years I feel less joy or distress
To hear water moving in wheel ruts, star-glintless,
                    *

And if any car comes now up that lane,
It carries nobody I could know,
And who wakes in that house now to hear the rain
May fall back to sleep—as I, long ago,
Who dreamed dawnward; and would rise to go.

III
THE WELL HOUSE

What happened there, it was not much,
But was enough. If you come back,
Not much may be *too much*, even if you have your old knack
Of stillness, and do not touch
A thing, a broken toy or rusted tool or any such
Object you happen to find
Hidden where, uncontrolled, grass and weeds bend.

The clematis that latches the door
Of the ruinous well house, you might break it.
Though guessing the water foul now, and not thirsting to take it,
With thirst from those years before
You might lean over the coping to stare at the water's dark-glinting floor.
Yes, that might be the event
To change *not much* to *too much*, and more than meant.

Yes, Truth is always in balance, and
Not much can become *too much* so quick.
Suppose you came back and found your heart suddenly sick,
And covered your sight with your hand:
Your tears might mean more than the thing you wept for but did not
                                        understand.

Yes, something might happen there
If you came back—even if you just stood to stare.

IV
IN MOONLIGHT, SOMEWHERE, THEY ARE SINGING

Under the maples at moonrise—
Moon whitening top leaf of the white oak
That rose from the dark mass of maples and range of eyes—
They were singing together, and I woke

From my sleep to the whiteness of moon-fire,
And deep from their dark maples, I
Could hear the two voices shake silver and free, and aspire
To be lost in moon-vastness of the sky.

My young aunt and her young husband
From their dark maples sang, and though
Too young to know what it meant I was happy and
So slept, for I knew I would come to know.

But what of the old man awake there,
As the voices, like vine, climbed up moonlight?
What thought did he think of past time as they twined bright in moon-air,
And veined, with their silver, the moon-flesh of night?

Far off, I recall, in the barn lot,
A mule stamped, once; but the song then
Was over, and for that night, or forever, would not
Resume—but should it again,

Now years later, wake me to white moon-fire
On pillow, high oak leaf, and far field,
I should hope to find imaged in whatever new voices aspire
Some faith in life yet, by my years, unrepealed.

V
DEBATE: QUESTION, QUARRY, DREAM

Asking what, asking what?—all a boy's afternoon,
Squatting in the canebrake where the muskrat will come.
Muskrat, muskrat, please now, please, come soon.
He comes, stares, goes, lets the question resume.
He has taken whatever answer may be down to his mud-burrow gloom.

Seeking what, seeking what?—foot soft in cedar-shade.
Was that a deer-flag white past windfall and fern?
No, but by bluffside lurk powers and in the fern glade
Tall presences, standing all night, like white fox-fire burn.
The small fox lays his head in your hand now and weeps
                               that you go, not to return.

Dreaming what, dreaming what?—lying on the hill at twilight,
The still air stirred only by moth wing, the last stain of sun
Fading to moth-sky, blood-red to moth-white and starlight,
And Time leans down to kiss the heart's ambition,
While far away, before moonrise, come the town lights, one by one.

Long since that time I have walked night streets, heel-iron
Clicking the stone, and in dark in windows have stared.
Question, quarry, dream—I have vented my ire on
My own heart that, ignorant and untoward,
Yearns for an absolute that Time would, I thought, have prepared,

But has not yet. Well, let us debate
The issue. But under a tight roof, clutching a toy,
My son now sleeps, and when the hour grows late,
I shall go forth where the cold constellations deploy
And lift up my eyes to consider more strictly the appalling logic of joy.

BALLAD:
BETWEEN THE BOXCARS

I
I CAN'T EVEN REMEMBER THE NAME

I can't even remember the name of the one who fell
Flat on his ass, on the cinders, between the boxcars.
I can't even remember whether he got off his yell
Before what happened had happened between the boxcars.

But whether or not he managed to get off his yell,
I remember its shape on his mouth, between the boxcars,
And it was shape that yours would be too if you fell
Flat on your ass, on the cinders, between the boxcars.

And there's one sure thing you had better remember well,
You go for the grip at the front, not the back, of the boxcars.
Miss the front, you're knocked off—miss the back, you never can tell
But you're flat on your ass, on the cinders, between the boxcars.

He was fifteen and old enough to know perfectly well
You go for the grip at the front, not the back, of the boxcars,
But he was the kind of smart aleck you always can tell
Will end flat on his ass, on the cinders, between the boxcars.

Suppose I remembered his name, then what the hell
Good would it do him now between the boxcars?
But it might mean something to me if I could tell
You the name of the one who fell between the boxcars.

II
HE WAS FORMIDABLE

He was formidable, he was, the little booger,
As he spat in his hands and picked up the Louisville Slugger,
And at that bat-crack
Around those bases he could sure ball the jack,
And if from the outfield the peg had beat him home,
He would slide in slick, like a knife in a nigger.
So we dreamed of an afternoon to come,
In the Series, the ninth-inning hush, in the Yankee Stadium,
Sun low, score tied, bases full, two out, and he'd waltz to the plate with
his grin—
But no, oh no, not now, not ever! for in
That umpireless rhubarb and steel-heeled hugger-mugger,
He got spiked sliding home, got spiked between the boxcars.

Oh, his hair was brown-bright as a chestnut, sun-glinting and curly,
And that lip that smiled boy-sweet could go, of a sudden, man-surly,
And the way he was built
Made the girls in his grade stare in darkness, and finger the quilt.
Yes, he was the kind you know born to give many delight,
And entering on such life-labor early,
Would have moved, bemused, in that rhythm and rite,
Through blood-throbbing blackness and moon-gleam
and pearly thigh-glimmer of night,
To the exquisite glut: *Woman Slays Self for Love*, as the tabloids would
tell—
But no, never now! Like a kid in his first brothel,
In that hot clasp and loveless hurly-burly,
He spilled, as boys may, too soon, between the boxcars.

Or, he might have managed the best supermarket in town,
Bright with banners and chrome, where housewives push carts up and
down,
And morning and night
Walked the street with his credit *A*-rated and blood pressure right,
His boy a dentist in Nashville, his girl at State Normal;
Or a scientist flushed with *Time*-cover renown

For vaccine, or bomb, or smog removal;
Or a hero with phiz like hewn cedar, though young for the stars of a
general,
Descending the steps of his personal plane to view the home-town
unveiling.
But no, never now!—battle-cunning, the test tube, retailing,
All, all, in a helter-skeltering mishmash thrown
    To that clobber and grind, too soon, between the boxcars.

But what is success, or failure, at the last?
The newspaper whirled down the track when the through freight has
passed
Will sink from that gust
To be of such value as it intrinsically must,
And why should we grieve for the name that boy might have made
To be printed on newsprint like that, for that blast
To whirl with the wheels' fanfaronade,
When we cannot even remember his name, nor humbly have prayed
That when that blunt grossness, slam-banging, bang-slamming, blots black
the last blue flash of sky,
And our own lips utter the crazed organism's cry,
We may know the poor self not alone, but with all who are cast
    To that clobber, and slobber, and scream, between the boxcars?

TWO STUDIES IN IDEALISM:
SHORT SURVEY OF AMERICAN,
AND HUMAN, HISTORY

For Allan Nevins

I
BEAR TRACK PLANTATION:
SHORTLY AFTER SHILOH

Two things a man's built for, killing and you-know-what.
As for you-know-what, I reckon I taken my share,
Bed-ease or bush-whack, but killing—hell, three's all I got,
And he promised me ten, Jeff Davis, the bastard. 'Taint fair.

It ain't fair, a man rides and knows he won't live forever,
And a man needs something to take with him when he dies.
Ain't much worth taking, but what happens under the cover
Or at the steel-point—yeah, that look in their eyes.

That same look, it comes in their eyes when you give 'em the business.
It's something a man can hang on to, come black-frost or sun.
Come hell or high water, it's something to save from the mess,
No matter whatever else you never got done.

For a second it seems like a man can know what he lives for,
When those eyelids go waggle, or maybe the eyes pop wide,
And that look comes there. Yeah, Christ, then you know who you are—
And will maybe remember that much even after you've died.

But now I lie worrying what look my own eyes got
When that Blue-Belly caught me off balance. Did my look mean then
That I'd honed for something not killing or you-know-what?
Hell, no. I'd lie easy if Jeff had just give me that ten.

II
HARVARD '61: BATTLE FATIGUE

I didn't mind dying—it wasn't that at all.
It behooves a man to prove manhood by dying for Right.
If you die for Right that fact is your dearest requital,
But you find it disturbing when others die who simply haven't the right.

Why should they die with that obscene insouciance?
They seem to insult the principle of your own death.
Touch pitch, be defiled: it was hard to keep proper distance
From such unprincipled wastrels of blood and profligates of breath.

I tried to slay without rancor, and often succeeded.
I tried to keep the heart pure, though my hand took stain.
But they made it so hard for me, the way they proceeded
To parody with their own dying that Death which only Right should
                                                           sustain.

Time passed. It got worse. It seemed like a plot against me.
I said they had made their own evil bed and lay on it,
But they grinned in the dark—they grinned—and I yet see
That last one. At woods-edge we held, and over the stubble they came
                                                           with bayonet.

He uttered his yell, he was there!—teeth yellow, some missing.
Why, he's old as my father, I thought, finger frozen on trigger.
I saw the ambeer on his whiskers, heard the old breath hissing.
The puncture came small on his chest. 'Twas nothing. The stain then got
                                                           bigger.

And he said: "Why, son, you done done it—I figgered I'd skeered ye."
Said: "Son, you look puke-pale. Buck up! If it hadn't been you,
Some other young squirt would a-done it." I stood, and weirdly
The tumult of battle went soundless, like gesture in dream. And I was
                                                           dead, too.

Dead, and had died for the Right, as I had a right to,
And glad to be dead, and hold my residence
Beyond life's awful illogic, and the world's stew,
Where people who haven't the right just die, with ghastly impertinence.

from

PROMISES
Poems 1954-1956

TO A LITTLE GIRL, ONE YEAR OLD, IN A RUINED FORTRESS

To Rosanna

I
SIROCCO

To a place of ruined stone we brought you, and sea-reaches.
Rocca: fortress, hawk-heel, lion-paw, clamped on a hill.
A hill, no. On a sea cliff, and crag-cocked, the embrasures
                                 commanding the beaches,
Range easy, with most fastidious mathematic and skill.

Philipus me fecit: he of Spain, the black-browed, the anguished,
For whom nothing prospered, though he loved God.
His arms, a great scutcheon of stone, once over the drawbridge,
                                 have languished
Now long in the moat, under garbage; at moat-brink, rosemary
                      with blue, thistle with gold bloom, nod.

Sun blaze and cloud tatter, now the sirocco, the dust swirl is swirled
Over the bay face, mounts air like gold gauze whirled; it traverses
                          the blaze-blue of water.
We have brought you where geometry of a military rigor survives
                        its own ruined world,
And sun regilds your gilt hair, in the midst of your laughter.

Rosemary, thistle, clutch stone. Far hangs Giannutri in blue air.
                       Far to that blueness the heart aches,
And on the exposed approaches the last gold of gorse bloom, in the
                               sirocco, shakes.

II
GULL'S CRY

White goose by palm tree, palm ragged, among stones the white oleander,
And the she-goat, brown, under pink oleanders, waits.
I do not think that anything in the world will move, not goat, not gander.
Goat droppings are fresh in the hot dust; not yet the beetle; the sun beats,

And under blue shade of the mountain, over blue-braiding sea-shadow,
The gull hangs white; whiter than white against the mountain-mass,
The gull extends motionless on a shelf of air, on the substance of shadow.
The gull, at an eye-blink, will, into the astonishing statement of sun, pass.

All night, next door, the defective child cried; now squats in the dust
         where the lizard goes.
The wife of the *gobbo* sits under vine leaves, she suffers, her eyes glare.
The engaged ones sit in the privacy of bemusement, heads bent: the
          classic pose.
Let the beetle work, the gull comment the irrelevant anguish of air,

But at your laughter let the molecular dance of the stone-dark
        glimmer like joy in the stone's dream,
And in that moment of possibility, let *gobbo, gobbo's* wife, and us, and all,
       take hands and sing: *redeem, redeem!*

III
THE CHILD NEXT DOOR

The child next door is defective because the mother,
Seven brats already in that purlieu of dirt,
Took a pill, or did something to herself she thought would not hurt,
But it did, and no good, for there came this monstrous other.

  *

The sister is twelve. Is beautiful like a saint.
Sits with the monster all day, with pure love, calm eyes.
Has taught it a trick, to make *ciao*, Italian-wise.
It crooks hand in that greeting. She smiles her smile without taint.

I come, and her triptych beauty and joy stir hate
—Is it hate?—in my heart. Fool, doesn't she know that the process
Is not that joyous or simple, to bless, or unbless,
The malfeasance of nature or the filth of fate?

Can it bind or loose, that beauty in that kind,
Beauty of benediction? We must trust our hope to prevail
That heart-joy in beauty be wisdom, before beauty fail
And be gathered like air in the ruck of the world's wind!

I think of your goldness, of joy, but how empires grind, stars are hurled.
I smile stiff, saying *ciao*, saying *ciao*, and think: *This is the world.*

IV
THE FLOWER

Above the beach, the vineyard
Terrace breaks to the seaward
Drop, where the cliffs fail
To a clutter of manganese shale.
Some is purple, some powdery-pale.
But the black lava-chunks stand off
The sea's grind, or indolent chuff.
The lava will withstand
The sea's beat, or insinuant hand,
And protect our patch of sand.

It is late. The path from the beach
Crawls up. I take you. We reach
The vineyard, and at that path angle

The hedge obtrudes a tangle
Of leaf and green bulge and a wrangle
Bee-drowsy and blowsy with white bloom,
Scarcely giving the passer-by room.
We know that the blossomy mass
Will brush our heads as we pass,
And at knee there's gold gorse and blue clover,
And at ankle, blue *malva* all over—
Plus plants I don't recognize
With my non-botanical eyes.
We approach, but before we get there,
If no breeze stirs that green lair,
The scent and sun-honey of air
Is too sweet comfortably to bear.

I carry you up the hill.
In my arms you are still.
We approach your special place,
And I am watching your face
To see the sweet puzzlement grow,
And then recognition glow.
Recognition explodes in delight.
You leap like spray, or like light.
Despite my arm's tightness,
You leap in gold-glitter and brightness.
You leap like a fish-flash in bright air,
And reach out. Yes, I'm well aware
That this is the spot, and hour,
For you to demand your flower.

When first we came this way
Up from the beach, that day
That seems now so long ago,
We moved bemused and slow
In the season's pulse and flow.
Bemused with sea, and slow
With June heat and perfume,
We paused here, and plucked you a bloom.
So here you always demand
Your flower to hold in your hand,

And the flower must be white,
For you have your own ways to compel
Observance of this ritual.
You hold it and sing with delight.
And your mother, for our own delight,
Picks one of the blue flowers there,
To put in your yellow hair.
That done, we go on our way
Up the hill, toward the end of the day.

But the season has thinned out.
From the bay edge below, the shout
Of a late bather reaches our ear,
Coming to the vineyard here
By more than distance thinned.
The bay is in shadow, the wind
Nags the shore to white.
The mountain prepares the night.

By the vineyard we have found
No bloom worthily white,
And the few we have found
Not distintegrated to the ground
Are by season and sea-salt browned.
We give the best one to you.
It is ruined, but will have to do.
Somewhat better the blue blossoms fare.
So we find one for your hair,
And you sing as though human need
Were not for perfection. We proceed
Past floss-borne or sloughed-off seed,
Past curled leaf and dry pod,
And the blue blossom will nod
With your head's drowsy gold nod.

Let all seasons pace their power,
As this has paced to this hour.
Let season and season devise
Their possibilities.
Let the future reassess

All past joy, and past distress,
Till we know Time's deep intent,
And the last integument
Of the past shall be rent
To show how all things bent
Their energies to that hour
When you first demanded your flower.

Yes, in that image let
Both past and future forget,
In clasped communal ease,
Their brute identities.

The path lifts up ahead
To the *rocca*, supper, bed.
We move in the mountain's shade.
The mountain is at our back.
But ahead, climbs the coast-cliff track.
The valley between is dim.
Ahead, on the cliff rim,
The *rocca* clasps its height.
It accepts the incipient night.

Just once we look back.
On sunset, a white gull is black.
It hangs over the mountain crest.
It hangs on that saffron west.
It makes its outcry.
It slides down the sky.

East now, it catches the light.
Its black has gone again white,
And over the *rocca's* height
It gleams in the last light.

Now it sinks from our sight.
Beyond the cliff is night.

It sank on unruffled wing.
We hear the sea rustling.

V
COLDER FIRE

It rained toward day. The morning came sad and white
With silver of sea-sadness and defection of season.
Our joys and convictions are sure, but in that wan light
We moved—your mother and I—in muteness of spirit past logical reason.

Now sun, afternoon, and again summer-glitter on sea.
As you to a bright toy, the heart leaps. The heart unlocks
Joy, though we know, shamefaced, the heart's weather should not be
Merely a reflex to a solstice, or sport of some aggrieved equinox.

No, the heart should be steadfast: I know that.
And I sit in the late-sunny lee of the watch-house,
At the fortress point, you on my knee now, and the late
White butterflies over gold thistle conduct their ritual carouse.

In whisperless carnival, in vehemence of gossamer,
Pale ghosts of pale passions of air, the white wings weave.
In tingle and tangle of arabesque, they mount light, pair by pair,
As though that tall light were eternal indeed, not merely the summer's
reprieve.

You leap on my knee, you exclaim at the sun-stung gyration.
And the upper air stirs, as though the vast stillness of sky
Had stirred in its sunlit sleep and made suspiration,
A luxurious languor of breath, as after love, there is a sigh.

But enough, for the highest sun-scintillant pair are gone
Seaward, past rampart and cliff borne, over blue sea-gleam.
Close to my chair, to a thistle, a butterfly sinks now, flight done.
By the gold bloom of thistle, white wings pulse under the sky's dream.

The sky's dream is enormous, I lift up my eyes.
In sunlight a tatter of mist clings high on the mountain-mass.
The mountain is under the sky, and there the gray scarps rise
Past paths where on their appointed occasions men climb, and pass.
*

Past grain-patch, last apron of vineyard, last terrace of olive,
Past chestnut, past cork grove, where the last carts can go,
Past camp of the charcoal maker, where coals glow in the black hive,
The scarps, gray, rise up. Above them is that place I know.

The pines are there, they are large, in a deep recess—
Shelf above scarp, enclave of rock, a glade
Benched and withdrawn in the mountain-mass, under the peak's duress.
We came there—your mother and I—and rested in that severe shade.

Pine-blackness mist-tangled, the peak black above: the glade gives
On the empty threshold of air, the hawk-hung delight
Of distance unspooled and bright space spilled—ah, the heart thrives!
We stood in that shade and saw sea and land lift in the far light.

Now the butterflies dance, time-tattered and disarrayed.
I watch them. I think how above that far scarp's sunlit wall
Mist threads in silence the darkness of boughs, and in that shade
Condensed moisture gathers at a needle-tip. It glitters, will fall.

I cannot interpret for you this collocation
Of memories. You will live your own life, and contrive
The language of your own heart, but let that conversation,
In the last analysis, be always of whatever truth you would live.

For fire flames but in the heart of a colder fire.
All voice is but echo caught from a soundless voice.
Height is not deprivation of valley, nor defect of desire,
But defines, for the fortunate, that joy in which all joys should rejoice.

PROMISES

To Gabriel

I
WHAT WAS THE PROMISE THAT SMILED FROM THE MAPLES AT EVENING?

What was the promise that smiled from the maples at evening?
Smiling dim from the shadow, recessed? What language of leaf-lip?
And the heels of the fathers click on the concrete, returning,
Each aware of his own unspecified burden, at sun-dip.
In first darkness hydrangeas float white in their spectral precinct.
Beneath pale hydrangeas the first firefly utters cold burning.
The sun is well down, the first star has now winked.

What was the promise when bullbats dizzied the sunset?
They skimmer and skitter in gold light at great height.
The guns of big boys on the common go *boom*, past regret.
Boys shout when the bullbat spins down in that gold light.
"Too little to shoot"—but next year you'll be a big boy.
So shout now and pick up the bird—why, that's blood, it is wet.
Its eyes are still open, your heart in the throat swells like joy.

What was the promise when, after the last light had died,
Children gravely, down walks, in spring dark, under maples, drew
Trains of shoe boxes, empty, with windows, with candles inside,
Going *chuck-chuck*, and blowing for crossings, lonely, *oo-oo?*
But on impulse you fled, and they called, called across the dark lawn,
Long calling your name, who now lay in the darkness to hide,
While the sad little trains glimmer on under maples, and on.

What was the promise when, after the dying was done,
All the long years before, like burnt paper, flared into black,
And the house shrunk to silence, the odor of flowers near gone?
Recollection of childhood was natural: cold gust at the back.

What door on the dark flings open, then suddenly bangs?
Yes, something was lost in between, but it's long, the way back.
You sleep, but in sleep hear a door that creaks where it hangs.

Long since, in a cold and coagulate evening, I've stood
Where they slept, the long dead, and the farms and far woods fled away,
And a gray light prevailed and both landscape and heart were subdued.
Then sudden, the ground at my feet was like glass, and I say
What I saw, saw deep down—with their fleshly habiliments rent,
But their bones in a phosphorus of glory agleam, there they lay,
Side by side, Ruth and Robert. But quickly that light was spent.

Earth was earth, and in earth-dark the glow died, therefore I lifted
My gaze to that world which had once been the heart's familiar,
Swell of woods and far field-sweep, in dusk by stream-gleams now wefted,
Railroad yonder and coal chute, town roofs far under the first star.
Then her voice, long forgotten, calm in silence, said: "Child."
And his, with the calm of a night field, or far star:
"We died only that every promise might be fulfilled."

II
COURT-MARTIAL

Under the cedar tree,
He would sit, all summer, with me:
An old man and small grandson
Withdrawn from the heat of the sun.

Captain, cavalry, C.S.A.,
An old man, now shrunken, gray,
Pointed beard clipped the classic way,
Tendons long gone crank and wry,
And long shrunken the cavalryman's thigh
Under the pale-washed blue jean.
His pipe smoke lifts, serene

Beneath boughs of the evergreen,
With sunlight dappling between.
I see him now, as once seen.

Light throbs the far hill.
The boughs of the cedar are still.

His years like landscape lie
Spread to the backward eye
In life's long irony.
All the old hoofbeats fade
In the calm of the cedar shade,
Where only the murmur and hum
Of the far farm, and summer, now come.
He can forget all—forget
Even mortgage and lien and debt,
Cutworm and hail and drouth,
Bang's disease, hoof-and-mouth,
Barn sagging and broken house.
Now in the shade, adrowse,
At last he can sit, or rouse
To light a pipe, or say to me
Some scrap of old poetry—
Byron or Burns—and idly
The words glimmer and fade
Like sparks in the dark of his head.

In the dust by his chair
I undertook to repair
The mistakes of his old war.
Hunched on that toy terrain,
Campaign by campaign,
I sought, somehow, to untie
The knot of History,
For in our shade I knew
That only the Truth is true,
That life is only the act
To transfigure all fact,
And life is only a story
And death is only the glory

Of the telling of the story,
And the *done* and the *to-be-done*
In that timelessness were one,
Beyond the poor *being done*.

The afternoon stood still.
Sun dazzled the far hill.

It was only a chance word
That a chance recollection had stirred.
"Guerrilla—what's that?" I said.
"Bushwhackers, we called 'em," he said.
"Were they on the Yankee side?"
"Son, they didn't have any side.
Just out to plunder and ride
And hell-rake the pore countryside.
Just out for themselves, so, son,
If you happened to run across one,
Or better, laid hand to a passel,
No need to be squeamish, or wrestle
Too long with your conscience. But if—"
He paused, raised his pipe, took a whiff—
"If your stomach or conscience was queasy,
You could make it all regular, easy.

"By the road, find some shade, a nice patch.
Even hackberry does, at a scratch.
Find a spring with some cress fresh beside it,
Growing rank enough to nigh hide it.
Lord, a man can sure thirst when you ride.
Yes, find you a nice spot to bide.
Bide sweet when you can when you ride.
Order halt, let the heat-daze subside.
Put your pickets, vedettes out, dismount.
Water horses, grease gall, take count,
And while the men rest and jaw,
You and two lieutenants talk law.
Brevitatem justitia amat.
Time is short—hell, a rope is—that's that."
                    *

That was that, and the old eyes were closed.
On a knee one old hand reposed,
Fingers crooked on the cob pipe, where
The last smoke raveled blue up the air.
Every tale ravels out to an end.
But smoke rose, did not waver or bend.
It unspooled, wouldn't stop, wouldn't end.

"By God—" and he jerked up his head.
"By God, they deserved it," he said.
"Don't look at me that way," he said.
"By God—" and the old eyes glared red.
Then shut in the cedar shade.

The head slept in that dusk the boughs made.
The world's silence made me afraid.
Then a July-fly, somewhere,
Like silk ripping, ripped the bright air.
Then stopped. Sweat broke in my hair.

I snatched my gaze away.
I swung to the blazing day.
Ruined lawn, raw house swam in light.
The far woods swam in my sight.
Throbbing, the fields fell away
Under the blaze of day.

Calmly then, out of the sky,
Blotting the sun's blazing eye,
He rode. He was large in the sky.
Behind, shadow massed, slow, and grew
Like cloud on the sky's summer blue.
Out of that shade-mass he drew.
To the great saddle's sway, he swung,
Not old now, not old now—but young,
Great cavalry boots to the thigh,
No speculation in eye.
Then clotting behind him, and dim,
Clot by clot, from the shadow behind him,

They took shape, enormous in air.
Behind him, enormous, they hung there:

Ornaments of the old rope,
Each face outraged, agape,
Not yet believing it true—
The hairy jaw askew,
Tongue out, out-staring eye,
And the spittle not yet dry
That was uttered with the last cry.

The horseman does not look back.
Blank-eyed, he continues his track,
Riding toward me there,
Through the darkening air.

The world is real. It is there.

III
GOLD GLADE

Wandering, in autumn, the woods of boyhood,
Where cedars, black, thick, rode the ridge,
Heart aimless as rifle, in boy-blankness of mood,
I came where the ridge broke, and a great ledge,
Limestone, set my toe high as treetops by the dark edge

Of a gorge, and water hid, grudging and grumbling,
And I saw, in my mind's eye, foam white on
Wet stone, stone wet-black, white water tumbling,
And so went down, and with some fright on
Slick boulders, crossed over. The gorge-depth drew night on,

But high beyond rock and leaf-lacing, the sky
Showed yet bright, and declivity wooed

My foot by the quietening stream, and so I
Went on, in quiet, through the beech wood:
There, in gold light, where the glade gave, it stood.

The glade was geometric, circular, gold,
No brush or weed breaking that bright gold of leaf-fall.
In the center it stood, absolute and bold
Beyond any heart-hurt, or eye's grief-fall.
Gold-massy the beech stood in that gold light-fall.

There was no stir of air, no leaf now gold-falling,
No tooth-stitch of squirrel, or any far fox-bark,
No woodpecker coding, or late jay calling.
Silence: above and below the gray bole's bark
The air was gold light. There could be no dark.

But of course dark came, and I can't recall
What county it was, for the life of me.
Montgomery, Todd, Christian—I know them all.
Was it even Kentucky or Tennessee?
Is it merely an image that keeps haunting me?

IV
DARK WOODS

1. TONIGHT THE WOODS ARE DARKENED

Tonight the woods are darkened.
 You have, long back, forgot
What impulse or perturbation
 Had made you rise. You went out

Of the house, where faces and light were,
 To walk, and the night was black.
The dog whined. He tried to follow.
 You picked up some rocks. Rocked him back.
  *

One yelp the brute gave from back there.
    Good. So now you were free
To enter the field and dark there
    Under your heart's necessity.

Under sparse star-gleam a glimmer
    Of pale dust provoked your feet
To pursue the ectoplasmic bisection
    Of the dark field-heave, and to meet,

Yonder where woods massed their darkness,
    A darkness more absolute.
All right: and in shadow the pale dust,
    How soundless, accepted the foot!

Foot trapped in that silken compulsion
    Of dust, and dust-softness, and the pale
Path's glimmer in the field-darkness,
    You moved. Did nerve fail?

Could you stop? No, all's re-enactment.
    Trapped in that *déjà-vu*,
Déjà-fait, *déjà-fait*, you hear whispers,
    In the dark, say, "Ah." Say: "You, too?"

Was there a field full of folk there,
    Behind you? Threading like mist?
All who, dark-hungry, once had flung forth
    From the house, and now persist

In the field-dark to spy on, then greet you—
    They who now rejoice not, nor grieve,
But yet leer in their spooky connivance,
    Waiting to pluck sleeve?

You wheel now to face them, but nothing
    Is there. Only you. And in starlight,
Beyond the old field and pale cow-track,
    The woods wait. They wait. *All right*.

2. THE DOGWOOD

All right: and with that wry acceptance you follow the cow-track.
Yes, it's dark in the woods, as black as a peddler's pocket.
Cobweb tangles, briar snatches. A sensible man would go back.
A bough finds your face, and one eye grieves in the socket.

Midnight compounds with the peeper. Now whippoorwills speak,
Far off. Then silence. What's that? And something blots star—
By your head velvet air-*whoosh*, a curdle and shudder of wing-creak.
It is only an owl. You go on. You can guess where you are.

For here is the gum-swamp, the slough where you once trapped the weasel.
Here the dead cow was dumped, and by buzzards duly divested.
All taint of mortality's long since wiped clean as a whistle.
Now love vine threads eyehole, God's peace is by violet attested.

The bones are long lost. In green grass the skull waits, has waited:
A cathedral for ants, and at noon, under white dome and transept,
They pass in green gloom, where sunlight's by leaf mitigated,
For leaf of the love vine shuts eyehole, as though the eye slept.

But now it's not noon, it is night, and ant-dark in that cow skull.
And man-dark in the woods. But go on, that's how men survive.
You went on in the dark, your heart tight as a nut in the hull.
Came back in the dark, and home, and throve as men thrive.

But not before you had seen it, sudden at a path-turn,
White-floating in darkness, the dogwood, white bloom in dark air.
Like an ice-break, broke joy; then you felt a strange wrath burn
To strike it, and strike, had a stick been handy in the dark there.

But one wasn't handy, so there on the path then, breath scant,
You stood, you stood there, and oh, could the poor heart's absurd
Cry for wisdom, for wisdom, ever be answered? Triumphant,
All night, the tree glimmered in darkness, and uttered no word.

3. THE HAZEL LEAF

Tonight the woods are darkened.
  You have forgotten what pain
Had once drawn you forth:
    To remember it might yet be some pain.
    But to forget may, too, be pain.

The hazel leaf falls in autumn.
  It slants athwart the gold air.
Boys come, prompt at nut-fall,
    To shout and kick up the gold leaves there.
    Shouts echo in high hickories not yet bare.

The hazel leaf falls in autumn.
  Boys go, and no voices intrude
Now at dusk-hour. The foot
    Of only the squirrel stirs leaf of this solitude.
    Otherwise, only shadow may now intrude.

The little green snake by the path-side,
  In May, lifts its jeweled head.
It stares, waves the tongue-wisp.
    What it hears on the path is not now your tread.
    But it still stares with lifted head.

Yes, your tread's now fainter and farther.
  Years muffle a tread, like grass.
Who passes, strikes; and now goes on.
    The snake waits, head crushed, to be observed by the next to pass.
    He will observe it, and then pass.

Tonight the woods are darkened.
  What other man may go there
Now stares, silent, breath scant,
    Waiting for the white petal to be released in dark air.
    Do not forget you were once there.

V
COUNTRY BURYING (1919)

A thousand times you've seen that scene:
   Oak grove, bare ground, little white church there,
Bone-white in that light, and through dust-pale green
   Of oak leaves, the steeple pokes up in the bright air.

For it is summer, and once I sat
   At grove-edge beyond the disarray
Of cars in the shade-patch, this way and that.
   They stood patient as mules now in the heat of the day.

Chevrolet, T-Model, a Hudson or two,
   They are waiting like me, and the afternoon glares.
Waiting is all they have come to do.
   What goes on inside is no concern of theirs,

Nor of mine, who have lost a boy's afternoon,
   When summer's so short, and half gone, just to bring
My mother to bury someone she'd scarce known.
   "I respect her," she'd said, but was that enough of a thing?

Who was she? Who knows? I'd not thought to ask it.
   That kind came to town, in buggy or Ford,
Some butter to swap, clutch of eggs in a basket,
   Gnarled hands in black mittens, old face yellow as a gourd.

It's no matter now who lies in the church,
   Where heads bend in duty in sparse rows.
Green miles of tobacco, sun-dazzled, stretch
   Away. Red clay, the road winds, goes on where it goes,

And we, too, now go, down the road, where it goes,
   My mother and I, the hole now filled.
Light levels in fields now, dusk crouches in hedgerows,
   As we pass from what is, toward what will be, fulfilled,
     *

237

And I passed toward voices and the foreign faces,
    Knew dawn in strange rooms, and the heart gropes for center,
But should I come back, back now where that place is,
    Oak grove, white church, in day-glare a-daze, I might enter.

For what? But enter, and find what I'd guess:
    The odor of varnish, hymnals stacked on a chair,
Light religiously dim by painted paper on window glass,
    And the insistent buzz of a fly lost in shadow, somewhere.

Why doesn't that fly stop buzzing—stop buzzing up there!

VI
SCHOOL LESSON BASED ON WORD OF
TRAGIC DEATH OF ENTIRE GILLUM FAMILY

They weren't so bright, or clean, or clever,
    And their noses were sometimes imperfectly blown,
But they always got to school the weather whatever,
    With old lard pail full of fried pie, smoked ham, and corn pone.

Tow hair was thick as a corn-shuck mat.
    They had milky blue eyes in matching pairs,
And barefoot or brogan, when they sat,
    Their toes were the kind that hook round the legs of chairs.

They had adenoids to make you choke,
    And buttermilk breath, and their flannels asteam,
And sat right mannerly while teacher spoke,
    But when book-time came their eyes were glazed and adream.

There was Dollie-May, Susie-May, Forrest, Sam, Brother—
    Thirteen down to eight the stairsteps ran.
They had popped right natural from their big fat mother—
    The clabber kind that can catch just by honing after a man.
        *

In town, Gillum stopped you, he'd say: "Say, mister,
   I'll name you what's true fer folks, ever-one.
Human-man ain't much more'n a big blood blister.
   All red and proud-swole, but one good squeeze and he's gone.

"Take me, ain't wuth lead and powder to perish,
   Just some spindle bone stuck in a pair of pants,
But a man's got his chaps to love and to cherish,
   And raise up and larn 'em so they kin git their chance."

So mud to the hub, or dust to the hock,
   God his helper, wet or dry,
Old Gillum swore by God and by cock,
   He'd git 'em larned before his own time came to die.

That morning blew up cold and wet,
   All the red-clay road was curdled as curd,
And no Gillums there for the first time yet.
   The morning drones on. Stove spits. Recess. Then the word.

Dollie-May was combing Susie-May's head.
   Sam was feeding, Forrest milking, got nigh through.
Little Brother just sat on the edge of his bed.
   Somebody must have said: "Pappy, now what you aimin' to do?"

An ice pick is a subtle thing.
   The puncture's small, blood only a wisp.
It hurts no more than a bad bee sting.
   When the sheriff got there the school-bread was long burned to a crisp.

In the afternoon silence the chalk would scrape.
   We sat and watched the windowpanes steam,
Blur the old corn field and accustomed landscape.
   Voices came now faint in our intellectual dream.

Which shoe—yes, which—was Brother putting on?
   That was something, it seemed, you just had to know.
But nobody knew, all afternoon,
   Though we studied and studied, as hard as we could, to know,
    *

Studying the arithmetic of losses,
    To be prepared when the next one,
By fire, flood, foe, cancer, thrombosis,
    Or Time's slow malediction, came to be undone.

We studied all afternoon, till getting on to sun.
There would be another lesson, but we were too young to take up that one.

VII
SUMMER STORM (CIRCA 1916), AND GOD'S GRACE

Toward sun, the sun flared suddenly red.
    The green of woods was doused to black.
    The cattle bellowed by the haystack.
Redder than ever, red clay was red.
    Up the lane the plowhands came pelting back.

Astride and no saddle, and they didn't care
    If a razor-back mule at a break-tooth trot
    Was not the best comfort a man ever got,
But came huddling on, with jangling gear,
    And the hat that jounced off stayed off, like as not.

In that strange light all distance died.
    You know the world's intensity.
    Field-far, you can read the aphid's eye.
The mole, in his sod, can no more hide,
    And weeps beneath the naked sky.

Past silence, sound insinuates
    Past ear into the inner brain.
    The toad's asthmatic breath is pain,
The cutworm's tooth grinds and grates,
    And the root, in earth, screams, screams again,
        *

But no cloud yet. No wind, though you,
  A half a county off, now spy
  The crow that, laboring zenith-high,
Is suddenly, with wings askew,
  Snatched, and tumbled down the sky.

And so you wait. You cannot talk.
  The creek-side willows shudder gray.
  The oak leaves turn the other way,
Gray as fish-belly. Then, with a squawk,
  The henhouse heaves, and flies away,

And darkness rides in on the wind.
  The pitchfork lightning tosses the trees,
  And God gets down on hands and knees
To peer and cackle and commend
  His own sadistic idiocies.

Next morning you stood where the bridge had washed out.
  A drowned cow bobbled down the creek.
  Raw-eyed, men watched. They did not speak.
Till one shrugged, said he guessed he'd make out.
  Then turned, took the woods-path up the creek.

VIII
FOUNDING FATHERS, NINETEENTH-CENTURY STYLE, SOUTHEAST U.S.A.

They were human, they suffered, wore long black coat and gold watch
                                                                chain.
They stare from daguerreotype with severe reprehension,
Or from genuine oil, and you'd never guess any pain
In those merciless eyes that now remark our own time's sad declension.
  *

Some composed declarations, remembering Jefferson's language.
Knew pose of the patriot, left hand in crook of the spine or
With finger to table, while the right invokes the Lord's just rage.
There was always a grandpa, or cousin at least, who had been a real Signer.

Some were given to study, read Greek in the forest, and these
Longed for an epic to do their own deeds right honor:
Were Nestor by pigpen, in some tavern brawl played Achilles.
In the ring of Sam Houston they found, when he died, one word
                                        engraved: *Honor.*

Their children were broadcast, like millet seed flung in a wind-flare.
Wives died, were dropped like old shirts in some corner of country.
Said, "Mister," in bed, the child-bride; hadn't known what to find there;
Wept all next morning for shame; took pleasure in silk; wore the keys to
                                        the pantry.

"Will die in these ditches if need be," wrote Bowie, at the Alamo.
And did, he whose left foot, soft-catting, came forward, and breath hissed:
Head back, gray eyes narrow, thumb flat along knife-blade, blade low.
"Great gentleman," said Henry Clay, "and a patriot." Portrait by
                                        Benjamin West.

Or take those, the nameless, of whom no portraits remain,
No locket or seal ring, though somewhere, broken and rusted,
In attic or earth, the long Decherd, stock rotten, has lain;
Or the mold-yellow Bible, God's Word, in which, in their strength,
                                        they also trusted.

Some wrestled the angel, and took a fall by the corncrib.
Fought the brute, stomp-and-gouge, but knew they were doomed
                                        in that glory.
All night, in sweat, groaned; fell at last with spit red and a cracked rib.
How sweet then the tears! Thus gentled, they roved the dark land with
                                        the old story.

Some prospered, had black men and acres, and silver on table,
But remembered the owl call, the smell of burnt bear fat on dusk-air.
Loved family and friends, and stood it as long as able—

"But money and women, too much is ruination, am Arkansas-bound."
                                                    So went there.

One of mine was a land shark, or so the book with scant praise
Denominates him. "A man large and shapeless,
Like a sack of potatoes set on a saddle," it says,
"Little learning but shrewd, not well trusted." Rides thus out of history,
                                        neck fat and napeless.

One fought Shiloh and such, got cranky, would fiddle all night.
The boys nagged for Texas. "God damn it, there's nothing, God damn it,
In Texas"—but took wagons, went, and to prove he was right,
Stayed a year and a day—"hell, nothing in Texas"—had proved it,
                                        came back to black vomit,

And died, and they died, and are dead, and now their voices
Come thin, like the last cricket in frost-dark, in grass lost,
With nothing to tell us for our complexity of choices,
But beg us only one word to justify their own old life-cost.

So let us bend ear to them in this hour of lateness,
And what they are trying to say, try to understand,
And try to forgive them their defects, even their greatness,
For we are their children in the light of humanness, and under the shadow
                                        of God's closing hand.

IX
FOREIGN SHORE, OLD WOMAN,
SLAUGHTER OF OCTOPUS

What now do the waves say
   To her, the old woman? She wears peasant black,
Alone on the beach, barefoot, and the day
   Withdraws, and she follows her slow track

Among volcanic black boulders, at sea-edge, and does not look back.
Sea-tongue softly utters among boulders by her track.

Saffron-saddening the mountain, the sun
   Sinks, and from sea, black boulder by boulder,
Night creeps. She stops by the boulders, leans on one;
   If from the black shawl she should unfold her
Old hand to the stone, she would find it yet warm, but it will be colder.
What has soft sea-tongue among black boulders told her?

All day there was picnic and laughter,
   Bright eye and hair tossing, white foam and thigh-flash,
And up from some cold coign and dark lair of water,
   Ectoplasmic, snot-gray, the obscene of the life-wish,
Sad tentacles weaving like prayer, eyes wide to glare-horror of day-wash,
The nightmare was spread out on stone. Boys yelled at the knife-flash.

The mountain is black, the sun drops.
   Among the black boulders, slow foam laces white.
Wind stirs, stirs paper of the picnic, stops,
   And agleam in imperial ease, at sky-height,
One gull hangs white in contempt of our human heart, and the night.
Pearl-slime of the slaughter, on black stone, glints in last light.

What can the sea tell her,
   That she does not now know, and know how to bear?
She knows, as the sea, that what came will recur,
   And detached in that wisdom, is aware
How grain by slow grain, the last sun heat from sand is expended on
                                   night air.
Bare flesh of an old foot knows that much, as she stands there.

This is not my country, or tongue,
   And my age not the old woman's age, or sea's age.
I shall go on my errand, and that before long,
   And leave much—but not, sea-darkling, her image,
Which in the day traffic, or as I stand in night dark, may assuage
The mind's pain of logic somewhat, or the heart's rage.

X
DARK NIGHT OF THE SOUL

Far off, two fields away,
Where dark of the river-woods lay,
I saw him divulged into daylight,
And stand to look left and right.
You could guess that quick look aside
Like a creature that knows how to hide
And does not debate pride.

Yes, the owner might come riding
With pistol in pocket, or striding
Along with a stout stick in hand,
To say: "Get the hell off my land!"
And the fellow would understand.

The owner would be justified
To clean him out, hoof-and-hide.
He might set your woods on fire,
Or at least mash down barbed wire.
That's all the excuse you require.

I was twelve, and my property sense
Was defective, though much improved since.
The day, anyway, was a scorcher,
So I didn't get up from the porch or
Even whistle the dogs from the shade
To provoke that flap-jawing parade
Of brute holler and whoop through the heat
To set a tooth in tramp-meat.
Didn't lay down my book, or even shout
Back into the house what was out,
How hedge-skulker and creature of night
And son of pellagra and spite
Now stood in our honest daylight.

There he stood, then slowly moved
One step. Stopped to see if he'd proved

That a man could survive half a minute
Outside the woods and not in it.
Looked back once to black safety of shade,
Then was caught in that great suction made
By the world's bright vacancy.
Was drawn by the world's blank eye.
Moved under the light-dizzy sky.

Far off, he is pin-prick size,
A mote dark in your dazzle of eyes.
He moves without truth or dimension
Across that vast space men should shun.
Lost and faceless and far,
Under light's malevolent stare,
In a painful retardation,
He moves toward what destination,
And so passes over
The enormity of clover.
Is now gone. Has passed over.

Now afternoon, strand by gold strand,
Raveled out, and over the land
Light leveled toward time set
For me to get up and forget
Egypt's arrogant dead
Or that Scaevola whom Rome bred.
Yes, I'd drop my book, and rouse
Myself and leave the house,
To go and round up the cows.

The cows drift up the lane.
White elder blooms by the lane.
I linger, leaf by leaf.
Dust, pale, powders the elder leaf,
And the pale, evening-idle sky
Drains your body light, and dry.
Air moves sweet through your husk under the sky.

But suddenly you are you,
No pale husk the air moves through.

My heart clenched hand-hard as I stood.
The adrenalin tingled my blood.
My lungs made a fish-gasp for air.
Cold prickles ran in my hair.
Beneath elder bloom, the eyes glare.

Couched under elder bloom,
In the honeysuckle he'd made room,
And the white strands regally wreathed
His old head, and the air he breathed
Was heavy with the languishment
Of that too sweet scent.
He was old, rough-grizzled, and spent.

Old and spent, but heaves up his head,
And our eyes thread the single thread
Of the human entrapment, until
A voice like a croak from an old well
Says: "Caint you git on away?"
But I simply can't move away.
Says: "Caint you let a man lay!"

I stared down the dank depth and heard
That croak from cold slime. Then he stirred,
Jerked up, stumbled up in his lair,
Like an old mule snagged on barbed wire.
Jerked free, and a moment stood there.

Then I was left standing alone
To stare down the lane where he'd gone.
He had gone, so I followed the cows
Up yonder toward the house,
There to enter and understand
My plate laid by a loving hand,
And to sleep, but not to understand
That somewhere on the dark land,
Unable to stop or stand,
On a track no man would have planned,
By age, rage, and rejection unmanned,
A bundle of rags in one hand,

His old black felt hat in the other hand,
At last he would understand.

Now his old head, bare,
Moves in the dark air.
It gleams with the absolute and glacial purity of despair.
It moves, and is touched by the unremitting glory of stars high
           in the night heavens there.
He moves in joy past contumely of stars or insolent indifference of
             the dark air.

May we all at last enter into that awfulness of joy he has found there.

XI
INFANT BOY AT MIDCENTURY

1. WHEN THE CENTURY DRAGGED
When the century dragged, like a great wheel stuck at dead center;
When the wind that had hurled us our half-century sagged now,
And only velleity of air somewhat snidely nagged now,
With no certain commitment to compass, or quarter: then you chose to
             enter.

You enter an age when the neurotic clock-tick
Of midnight competes with the heart's pulsed assurance of power.
You have entered our world at scarcely its finest hour,
And smile now life's gold Apollonian smile at a sick dialectic.

You enter at the hour when the dog returns to his vomit,
And fear's moonflower spreads, white as girl-thigh, in our dusk of
             compromise;
When posing for pictures, arms linked, the same smile in their eyes,
Good and Evil, to iron out all differences, stage their meeting at summit.
 *

You come in the year when promises are broken,
And petal fears the late, as fruit the early frost-fall;
When the young expect little, and the old endure total recall,
But discover no logic to justify what they had taken, or forsaken.

But to take and forsake now you're here, and the heart will compress
Like stone when we see that rosy heel learn,
With its first step, the apocalyptic power to spurn
Us, and our works and days, and onward, prevailing, pass

To pause, in high pride of unillusioned manhood,
At the gap that gives on the new century, and land,
And with calm heart and level eye command
That dawning perspective and possibility of human good.

2 . MODIFICATION OF LANDSCAPE
There will, indeed, be modification of landscape,
And in margin of natural disaster, substantial reduction.
There will be refinement of principle, and purified action,
And expansion, we trust, of the human heart-hope, and hand-scope.

But is it a meanness of spirit and indulgence of spite
To suggest that your fair time, and friends, will mirror our own,
And ourselves, for the flesh will yet grieve on the bone,
And the heart need compensation for its failure to study delight?

Some will take up religion, some discover the virtue of money.
Some will find liberal causes the mask for psychic disturbance.
Some will expiate ego with excessive kindness to servants,
And some make a cult of honor, though having quite little, if any.

Some, hating all humans, will cultivate love for cats,
And some from self-hate will give children a morbid devotion.
Some will glorify friendship, but watch for the slightest motion
Of eyelid, or lip-twitch, and the longed-for betrayal it indicates.

Success for the great will be heart-bread, and the soul's only ease.
For some it will stink, like mackerel shining in moonlight.

At the mere thought of failure some will wet their sheets in the night,
Though some wear it proud as a medal, or manhood's first social disease.

The new age will need the old lies, as our own more than once did;
For death is ten thousand nights—yes, it's only the process
Of accommodating flesh to idea, but there's natural distress
In learning to face Truth's glare-glory, from which our eyes are long hid.

3. BRIGHTNESS OF DISTANCE

You will read the official histories—true, no doubt.
Barring total disaster, the record will speak from the shelf.
And if there's disaster, disaster will speak for itself.
So all of our lies will be truth, and the truth vindictively out.

Remember our defects, we give them to you gratis.
But remember that ours is not the worst of times.
Our country's convicted of follies rather than crimes—
We throw out baby with bath, drop the meat in the fire where the fat is.

And in even such stew and stink as Tacitus
Once wrote of, his generals, gourmets, pimps, poltroons,
He found persons of private virtue, the old-fashioned stout ones
Who would bow the head to no blast; and we know that such are yet
> with us.

He was puzzled how virtue found perch past confusion and wrath;
How even Praetorian brutes, blank of love, as of hate,
Proud in their craftsman's pride only, held a last gate,
And died, each back unmarred as though at the barracks bath.

And remember that many among us wish you well;
And once, on a strange shore, an old man, toothless and through,
Groped a hand from the lattice of personal disaster to touch you.
He sat on the sand for an hour; said *ciao, bello*, as evening fell.

And think, as you move past our age that grudges and grieves,
How eyes, purged of envy, will follow your sunlit chance.
Eyes will brighten to follow your brightness and dwindle of distance.
From privacy of fate, eyes will follow, as though from the shadow of
> leaves.

XII
LULLABY: SMILE IN SLEEP

Sleep, my son, and smile in sleep.
You will dream the world anew.
Watching you now sleep,
I feel the world's depleted force renew,
Feel the nerve expand and knit,
Feel a rustle in the blood,
Feel wink of warmth and stir of spirit,
As though spring woke in the heart's cold underwood.
The vernal work is now begun.
Sleep, my son.
Sleep, son.

You will see the nestling fall.
Blood flecks grass of the rabbit form.
You will, of course, see all
The world's brute ox-heel wrong, and shrewd hand-harm.
Throats are soft to invite the blade.
Truth invites the journalist's lie.
Love bestowed mourns trust betrayed,
But the heart most mourns its own infidelity.
The greater, then, your obligation.
Dream perfection.
Dream, son.

When the diver leaves the board
To hang at gleam-height against the sky,
Trajectory is toward
An image hung perfect as light in his mind's wide eye.
So your dream will later serve you.
So now, dreaming, you serve me,
And give our hope new patent to
Enfranchise human possibility.
Grace undreamed is grace forgone.
Dream grace, son.
Sleep on.
            *

Dream that sleep is a sunlit meadow
Drowsy with a dream of bees
Threading sun, and the shadow
Where you lie lulled by their sunlit industries.
Let the murmurous bees of sleep
Tread down honey in the honeycomb.
Heart-deep now, your dream will keep
Sweet in that deep comb for time to come.
Dream the sweetness coming on.
Dream, sweet son.
Sleep on.

What if angry vestors veer
Around your sleeping head, and form?
There's never need to fear
Violence of the poor world's abstract storm.
For now you dream Reality.
Matter groans to touch your hand.
Matter lifts now like the sea
Toward that cold moon that is your dream's command.
Dream the power coming on.
Dream, strong son.
Sleep on.

XIII
MAN IN MOONLIGHT

1. MOONLIGHT OBSERVED FROM RUINED FORTRESS
Great moon, white-westering past our battlement,
Dark sea offers silver scintillance to your sky,
And not less responsive would my human heart be if I
Had been duly instructed in what such splendors have meant.

I have thought on the question by other sea, other shore:
When you smoothed the sweet Gulf asleep, like a babe at the breast,

When the moon-lashed old freighter banged stars in Atlantic unrest,
When you spangled spume-tangle on black rock, and seals barked at
                                                            sea-roar.

Décor must be right, of course, for your massive effect,
But a Tennessee stock-pond is not beneath your contempt,
Though its littoral merely a barnyard with cow-pats, unkempt.
Yes, to even a puddle you've been known to pay some respect.

And once on the Cumberland's bluffs I stood at midnight,
With music and laughter behind me, while my eyes
Were trapped in gleam-glory, but the heart's hungry surmise
Faded. So back to the racket and bottle's delight.

Be it sea or a sewer, we know you have never much cared
What sort of excuse, just so you may preen and prink,
With vulgarities to make Belasco blink
And tricks that even Houdini wouldn't have dared.

So now with that old, anguishing virtuosity
You strike our cliff, and then lean on to Carthage.
We stand on the crumbling stone and ruins of rage,
To watch your Tyrrhenian silver prank the sea.

And so we enact again the compulsive story,
Knowing of course the end—and ah, how soon—
But caught in that protocol of plenilune
And our werewolf thirst to drink the blood of glory.

We stare, we stare, but will not stare for long.
You will not tell us what we need to know.
Our feet soon go the way that they must go,
In diurnal dust and heat, and right and wrong.

2 .   WALK BY MOONLIGHT IN SMALL TOWN
Through the western window full fell moonlight.
It must have waked me where I lay.
Room objects swam in that spooky day.

I rose, dressed, walked the summer night,
As long years back I had moved in that compulsive light.

Lawns, green by day, now shimmered like frost.
Shadow, beast-black, in porches lurked.
On house fronts, windowpanes moon-smirked.
Past supper, paper read, lawn hosed,
How white, in the depth of dark rooms now, faces reposed.

Down Main Street, the window dummies blessed,
With lifted hand and empty stare,
The glimmering emptiness of air,
As though lunatically to attest
What hope the daylight heart might reasonably have possessed.

Three boxcars slept, as quiet as cows.
They were so tired, they'd been so far.
SP and *Katy*, *L & N R R*—
After bumble and bang, and where God knows,
They'd cracked the rust of a weed-rank spur, for this pale repose.

Long, long ago, at night, up that track,
I had watched the Pullman flash and fade,
Then heard, in new quiet, the beat my heart made.
But every ticket's round-trip; now back,
I stood and again watched night-distance flee up that empty track.

I crossed the track, walked up the rise.
The school building hulked, ugly as day.
Beyond, the night fields fell away.
Building and grounds had shrunk in size,
And that predictable fact seemed pitiful to my eyes.

And pitiful was the moon-bare ground.
Dead grass, the gravel, earth ruined and raw—
It had not changed. And then I saw
That children were playing, with no sound.
They ceased their play, then quiet as moonlight, drew, slow, around.
                *

Their eyes were fixed on me, and I
Now tried, face by pale face, to find
The names that haunted in my mind.
Each small, upgazing face would lie
Sweet as a puddle, and silver-calm, to the night sky.

But something grew in their pale stare:
Not reprobation or surprise,
Nor even forgiveness in their eyes,
But a humble question dawning there,
From face to face, like beseechment dawning on empty air.

Might a man but know his Truth, and might
He live so that life, by moon or sun,
In dusk or dawn, would be all one—
Then never on a summer night
Need he stand and shake in that cold blaze of Platonic light.

3. LULLABY: MOONLIGHT LINGERS

Moonlight lingers down the air.
Moonlight marks the window-square
As I stand and watch you sleep.
I hear the rustle where
The sea stirs sweet and sighs in its silvered sleep.
My son, sleep deep.
Sleep deep, son, and dream how moonlight
Unremitting, whitely, whitely, unpetals down the night.
As you sleep, now moonlight
Mollifies the mountain's rigor,
Laves the olive leaf to silver,
And black on the moon-pale trunk of the olive
Prints the shadow of an olive leaf.
Sleep, let moonlight give
That dark secondary definition to the olive leaf.
Sleep, son, past grief.

Now I close my eyes and see
Moonlight white on a certain tree.
It was a big white oak near a door

Familiar, long back, to me,
But now years unseen, and my foot enters there no more.
My son, sleep deep.
Sleep deep, son, and let me think
How a summer lane glimmers in moonlight to the cedar woods' dark brink.
Sleep, and let me now think
Of moon-frost white on the black boughs of cedar,
White moon-rinse on meadow, whiter than clover,
And at moon-dark stone, how water woke
In a wink of glory, then slid on to sleep.
Sleep, let this moon provoke
Moonlight more white on that landscape lost in the heart's homely deep.
Son, past grief, sleep.

Moonlight falls on sleeping faces.
It fell in far times and other places.
Moonlight falls on your face now,
And now in memory's stasis
I see moonlight mend an old man's Time-crossed brow.
My son, sleep deep,
For moonlight will not stay.
Now moves to seek that empty pillow, a hemisphere away.
Here, then, you'll be waking to the day.
Those who died, died long ago,
Faces you will never know,
Voices you will never hear—
Though your father heard them in the night,
And yet, sometimes, I can hear
Their utterance like the rustling tongue of a pale tide in moonlight:
Sleep, son. Good night.

MAD YOUNG ARISTOCRAT ON BEACH

He sits in blue trunks on the sand, and children sing.
Their voices are crystal and sad, and tinkle in sunlight.
Their voices are crystal, and the tinkling
Of sadness, like gold ants, crawls on his quivering heart in its midnight.
And the sea won't be still, won't be still,
In that freaking and fracture and dazzle of light.
Yes, somebody ought to take steps and stop it.
It's high time that somebody did, and he thinks that he will.
Why, it's simple, it's simple, just get a big mop and mop it,
Till it's dry as a bone—you sea, you *cretino*, be still!
But he's tired, he is tired, and wants only sleep.
Oh, Lord, let us pray that the children stop singing before he begins to
weep.

If he wept, we just couldn't bear it, but look, he is smiling!
He ponders how charming it is to smile, and magnanimous.
And his smile, indeed, is both sweet and beguiling,
And joy floods his heart now like hope, to replace that old dark animus.
So look! at the great concert grand,
He is bowing, and bowing, and smiling now on us,
And smiles at the sea, at the sea's bright applause—
But fame, ah, how sad! Again he sits on the sand,
And thinks how all human rewards are but gauds and gewgaws,
And lets sand, grain by grain, like history slip from his hand.
But his mother once said that his smile was sweet.
Curse the bitch, it is power man wants, and like a black cloud now mounts
to his feet.

He is young and sun-brown and tall and well formed, and he knows it.
He will swim in the sea, the water will break to his will.
Now emerging on shore, he is lethal, he shows it.
Yes, let them beware that brute jaw-jut and eye cold now and still.
And let him beware, beware—
That brother, the elder, who comes to the title.
But a title, *merde!* he will marry a passport,
And dollars, of course—he has blood, though he isn't the heir.

Then sudden as death, a thought stops him chillingly short:
Mais l'Amérique, merde! why it's full of Americans there.
So closes his eyes, longs for home, longs for bed.
Ah, that sweet-haunched new housemaid! But knows he can't get her
                                        except in the dark of his head.

So thinks of a whore he once had: she was dull as a sow,
And not once, never once, showed affection. He thinks he will cry.
Then thinks, with heart sweet, he'll be dead soon now,
And opens his eyes to the blaze and enormousness of the sky.
And we watch him, we watch him, and we
Are lonely, are lonely as death, though we try
To love him, but can't, for we sit on the sand,
And eyes throb at the merciless brilliance and bicker of sea,
While sand, grain by grain, like our history, slips from his hand.
We should love him, because his flesh suffers for you and for me,
As our own flesh should suffer for him, and for all
Who will never come to the title, and be loved for themselves, at
                                        innocent nightfall.

XV
DRAGON COUNTRY: TO JACOB BOEHME

This is the dragon's country, and these his own streams.
The slime on the railroad rails is where he has crossed the track.
On a frosty morning, that field mist is where his great turd steams,
And there are those who have gone forth and not come back.

I was only a boy when Jack Simms reported the first depredation,
What something had done to his hog pen. They called him a God-damn
                                        liar.
Then said it must be a bear, after some had viewed the location,
With fence rails, like matchwood, splintered, and earth a bloody mire.
    *

But no bear had been seen in the county in fifty years, they knew.
It was something to say, merely that, for people compelled to explain
What, standing in natural daylight, they couldn't believe to be true;
And saying the words, one felt in the chest a constrictive pain.

At least, some admitted this later, when things had got to the worst—
When, for instance, they found in the woods the wagon turned on its side,
Mules torn from trace chains, and you saw how the harness had burst.
Spectators averted the face from the spot where the teamster had died.

But that was long back, in my youth, just the first of case after case.
The great hunts fizzled. You followed the track of disrepair,
Ruined fence, blood-smear, brush broken, but came in the end to a place
With weed unbent and leaf calm—and nothing, nothing, was there.

So what, in God's name, could men think when they couldn't bring to bay
That belly-dragging earth-evil, but found that it took to air?
Thirty-thirty or buckshot might fail, but then at least you could say
You had faced it—assuming, of course, that you had survived the affair.

We were promised troops, the Guard, but the Governor's skin got thin
When up in New York the papers called him Saint George of Kentucky.
Yes, even the Louisville reporters who came to Todd County would grin.
Reporters, though rarely, still come. No one talks. They think it unlucky.

If a man disappears—well, the fact is something to hide.
The family says, gone to Akron, or up to Ford, in Detroit.
When we found Jebb Johnson's boot, with the leg, what was left, inside,
His mother said, no, it's not his. So we took it out to destroy it.

Land values are falling, no longer do lovers in moonlight go.
The rabbit, thoughtless of air gun, in the nearest pasture cavorts.
Now certain fields go untended, the local birth rate goes low.
The coon dips his little black paw in the riffle where he nightly resorts.

Yes, other sections have problems somewhat different from ours.
Their crops may fail, bank rates rise, loans at rumor of war be called,
But we feel removed from maneuvers of Russia, or other great powers,
And from much ordinary hope we are now disenthralled.

*

The Catholics have sent in a mission, Baptists report new attendance.
But all that's off the point! We are human, and the human heart
Demands language for reality that has not the slightest dependence
On desire, or need—and in church fools pray only that the Beast depart.

But if the Beast were withdrawn now, life might dwindle again
To the ennui, the pleasure, and the night sweat, known in the time before
Necessity of truth had trodden the land, and our hearts, to pain,
And left, in darkness, the fearful glimmer of joy, like a spoor.

XVI
BALLAD OF A SWEET DREAM OF PEACE

1. AND DON'T FORGET YOUR CORSET COVER,
     EITHER

And why, in God's name, is that elegant bureau
Standing out here in the woods and dark?
Because, in God's name, it would create a furor
If such a Victorian piece were left in the middle of Central Park,
To corrupt the morals of young and old
With its marble top and drawer pulls gilt gold
And rosewood elaborately scrolled,
And would you, in truth, want your own young sister to see it in the Park?
But she knows all about it, her mother has told her,
And besides, these days, she is getting much older,
And why, in God's name, is that bureau left in the woods?
All right, I'll tell you why.
It has as much right there as you or I,
For the woods are God's temple, and even a bureau has moods.
But why, in God's name, is that elegant bureau left all alone in the woods?

It is left in the woods for the old lady's sake,
For there's privacy here for a household chore,

And Lord, I can't tell you the time it can take
To apply her own mixture of beeswax and newt-oil to bring out the gloss
once more.

For the poor old hands move slower each night,
And can't manage to hold the cloth very tight,
And it's hard without proper light.
But why, in God's name, all this privacy for a simple household chore?
In God's name, sir! would you simply let
Folks see how naked old ladies can get?
Then let the old bitch buy some clothes like other folks do.
She once had some clothes, I am told,
But they're long since ruined by the damp and mold,
And the problem is deeper when bones let the wind blow through.
Besides it's not civil to call her a bitch—and her your own grandma, too.

2 . K E E P S A K E S

Oh, what brings her out in the dark and night?
She has mislaid something, just what she can't say,
But something to do with the bureau, all right.
Then why, in God's name, does she polish so much, and not look
in a drawer right away?
Every night, in God's name, she does look there,
But finds only a Book of Common Prayer,
A ribbon-tied lock of gold hair,
A bundle of letters, some contraceptives, and an orris-root sachet.
Well, what is the old fool hunting for?
Oh, nothing, oh, nothing that's in the top drawer,
For that's left by late owners who had their own grief to withstand,
And she tries to squinch and frown
As she peers at the Prayer Book upside down,
And the contraceptives are something she can't understand,
And oh, how bitter the tears she sheds, with some stranger's old letters
in hand!

You're lying, you're lying, she can't shed a tear!
Not with eyeballs gone, and the tear ducts, too.
You are trapped in a vulgar error, I fear,
For asleep in the bottom drawer is a thing that may prove instructive to
you:

*

Just an old-fashioned doll with a china head,
And a cloth body naked and violated
By a hole through which sawdust once bled,
But drop now by drop, on a summer night, from her heart it is treacle
bleeds through.

In God's name, what!—Do I see her eyes move?
Of course, and she whispers, "I died for love,"
And your grandmother whines like a dog in the dark and shade,
For she's hunting somebody to give
Her the life they had promised her she would live,
And I shudder to think what a stink and stir will be made
When some summer night she opens the drawer and finds that poor
self she'd mislaid.

3. GO IT, GRANNY—GO IT, HOG!

Out there in the dark, what's that horrible chomping?
Oh, nothing, just hogs that forage for mast,
And if you call, "Hoo-pig!" they'll squeal and come romping,
For they'll know from your voice you're the boy who slopped them
in dear, dead days long past.

Any hogs that I slopped are long years dead,
And eaten by somebody and evacuated,
So it's simply absurd, what you said.
You fool, poor fool, all Time is a dream, and we're all one Flesh, at last,
And the hogs know that, and that's why they wait,
Though tonight the old thing is a little bit late,
But they're mannered, these hogs, as they wait for her creaky old tread.
Polite, they will sit in a ring,
Till she finishes work, the poor old thing:
Then old bones get knocked down with a clatter to wake up the dead,
And it's simply absurd how loud she can scream with no shred of a tongue
in her head.

4. FRIENDS OF THE FAMILY, OR BOWLING A
STICKY CRICKET

Who else, in God's name, comes out in these woods?
Old friends of the family, whom you never saw,

Like yon cranky old coot, who mumbles and broods,
With yachting cap, rusty frock coat, and a placard proclaiming, "I am
                                                                    the Law!"
What makes him go barefoot at night in God's dew?
In God's name, you idiot, so would you
If you'd suffered as he had to
When expelled from his club for the horrible hobby that taught him the
                                                                nature of law.

They learned that he drowned his crickets in claret.
The club used cologne, and so couldn't bear it.
But they drown them in claret in Buckingham Palace!
Fool, law is inscrutable, so
Barefoot in dusk and dew he must go,
And at last each cries out in a dark stone-glimmering place,
"I have heard the voice in the dark, seeing not who utters. Show me
                                                                Thy face!"

5. YOU NEVER KNEW HER EITHER, THOUGH YOU THOUGHT YOU DID

Why now, in God's name, is the robe de nuit
Of that girl so torn, and what is that stain?
It's only dried blood, in God's name, that you see.
But why does she carry that leaf in her hand? Will you try, in God's
                                                            name, to explain?

It's a burdock leaf under which she once found
Two toads in coitu on the bare black ground,
So now she is nightly bound
To come forth to the woods to embrace a thorn tree, to try to understand
                                                                    pain,

And then wipes the blood on her silken hair,
And cries aloud, "Oh, we need not despair,
For I bleed, oh, I bleed, and God lives!" And the heart may stir
Like water beneath wind's tread
That wanders whither it is not said.
Oh, I almost forgot—will you please identify her?
She's the afternoon one who to your bed came, lip damp, the breath like
                                                                    myrrh.

6. I GUESS YOU OUGHT TO KNOW WHO YOU ARE

Could that be a babe crawling there in night's black?
Why, of course, in God's name, and birth-blind, but you'll see
How to that dead chestnut he'll crawl a straight track,
Then give the astonishing tongue of a hound with a coon treed up in a tree.
Well, who is the brat, and what's he up to?
He's the earlier one that they thought would be you,
And perhaps, after all, it was true,
For it's hard in these matters to tell sometimes. *But look, in God's name,*

I am me!

If you are, there's the letter a hog has in charge,
With a gold coronet and your own name writ large,
And in French, most politely, "Répondez s'il vous plaît."
Now don't be alarmed we are late.
What's time to a hog? We'll just let them wait.
But for when you are ready, our clients usually say
That to shut the eyes tight and get down on the knees is the quickest and

easiest way.

7. RUMOR UNVERIFIED STOP CAN YOU
CONFIRM STOP

Yes, clients report it the tidiest way,
For the first time at least, when all is so strange
And the helpers get awkward sometimes with delay.
But later, of course, you can try other methods that fancy suggests you

arrange.

There are clients, in fact, who, when ennui gets great,
Will struggle, or ingeniously irritate
The helpers to acts I won't state:
For Reality's all, and to seek it, some welcome, at whatever cost, any

change.

But speaking of change, there's a rumor astir
That the woods are sold, and the Purchaser
Soon comes, and if credulity's not now abused,
Will, on this property, set
White foot-arch familiar to violet,
And heel that, smiting stone, is not what is bruised,
And subdues to sweetness the pathside garbage, or thing body had refused.

XVII

BOY'S WILL, JOYFUL LABOR WITHOUT PAY, AND HARVEST HOME (1918)

1 . MORNING

By breakfast time the bustle's on.
In the field the old red thresher clatters.
The old steam tractor shakes and batters.
Sweat pops already in the hot sun.
The dogs are barking, mad as hatters.

You bolt your oatmeal, up and go.
The world is panting, the world won't wait.
All energy's unregenerate.
Blood can't abide the status quo.
You run as far as the front gate,

Then stop. For when your hope is displayed
To wait you, you must feast the eye
An instant on possibility,
Before finite constriction is made
To our pathos of rapacity.

2 . WORK

The hand that aches for the pitchfork heft
Heaves a sheaf from the shock's rich disrepair.
The wagoner snags it in mid-air,
Says, "Boy, save yore strength, 'fore you got none left,"
And grins, then wipes the sweat from his hair.

3 . THE SNAKE

Daylong, light, gold, leans on the land.
You stoke the tractor. You *gee* and *haw*.
You feed the thresher's gap-toothed maw.
Then on a load-top, high, you stand
And see your shadow, black as law,

*

Stretch far now on the gold stubble.
By now breath's short. Sweat stings the eyes.
Blue denim is sweat-black at the thighs.
If you make a joke, you waste your trouble.
In that silence the shout rings with surprise.

When you wreck a shock, the spot below
Is damp and green with a vernal gloom.
Field mouse or rabbit flees its doom,
And you scarcely notice how they go.
But a black snake rears big in his ruined room.

Defiant, tall in that blast of day,
Now eye for eye, he swaps his stare.
His outrage glitters on the air.
Men shout, ring around. He can't get away.
Yes, they are men, and a stone is there.

Against the wounded evening matched,
Snagged high on a pitchfork tine, he will make
Slow arabesques till the bullbats wake.
An old man, standing stooped, detached,
Spits once, says, "Hell, just another snake."

4. HANDS ARE PAID

The thresher now has stopped its racket.
It waits there small by the stack it has made.
The work is done, the hands are paid.
The silver dollar's in the sweat-cold pocket,
And the shirt sticks cold to the shoulder blade.

Out of the field, the way it had come,
Dragging the thresher's list and bumble,
The tractor now, a-clank, a-shamble,
Grunts down the pike, the long way home.
In dusk, to water now, mules, slow, amble.

The dollar glints on the mantel shelf.
By the coal-oil lamp the man leans his head

Over fried sowbelly and cold corn bread.
He's too sleepy now to wash himself.
Kicks off his brogans. Gets to bed.

The bullbat has come, long back, and gone.
White now, the evening star hangs to preside
Over woods and dark water and far countryside.
The little blood that smeared the stone
Dropped in the stubble, has long since dried.

The springs of the bed creak now, and settle.
The overalls hang on the back of a chair
To stiffen, slow, as the sweat gets drier.
Far, under a cedar, the tractor's metal
Surrenders last heat to the night air.

In the cedar dark a white moth drifts.
The mule's head, at the barn-lot bar,
Droops sad and saurian under night's splendor.
In the star-pale field, the propped pitchfork lifts
Its burden, hung black, to the white star,

And the years go by like a breath, or eye-blink,
And all history lives in the head again,
And I shut my eyes and I see that scene,
And name each item, but cannot think
What, in their urgency, they must mean,

But know, even now, on this foreign shore,
In blaze of sun and the sea's stare,
A heart-stab blessed past joy or despair,
As I see, in the mind's dark, once more,
That field, pale, under starlit air.

XVIII
LULLABY: A MOTION LIKE SLEEP

Under the star and beech-shade braiding,
Past the willow's dim solicitudes,
Past hush of oak-dark and a stone's star-glinted upbraiding,
Water moves, in a motion like sleep,
Along the dark edge of the woods.
So, son, now sleep.

Sleep, and feel how now, at woods-edge,
The water, wan, moves under starlight,
Before it finds that dark of its own deepest knowledge,
And will murmur, in motion like sleep,
In that leaf-dark languor of night.
So, son, sleep deep.

Sleep, and dream how deep and dreamless
The covered courses of blood are:
And blood, in a motion like sleep, moves, gleamless,
By alleys darkened deep now
In the leafage of no star.
So, son, sleep now.

Sleep, for sleep and stream and blood-course
Are a motion with one name,
And all that flows finds end but in its own source,
And a circuit of motion like sleep,
And will go as once it came.
So, son, now sleep

Till the clang of cock-crow, and dawn's rays,
Summon your heart and hand to deploy
Their energies to know, in the excitement of day-blaze,
How like a wound, and deep,
Is Time's irremediable joy.
So, son, now sleep.

from

SELECTED POEMS

1923-1943

THE BALLAD OF BILLIE POTTS

(When I was a child I heard this story from an old lady who was a relative of mine. The scene, according to her version, was in the section of Western Kentucky known as "Between the Rivers," the region between the Cumberland and the Tennessee. The name of Bardstown in the present account refers to Bardstown, Kentucky, where the first race track west of the mountains was laid out late in the eighteenth century.)

Big Billie Potts was big and stout
In the land between the rivers
His shoulders were wide and his gut stuck out
Like a croker of nubbins and his holler and shout
Made the bob-cat shiver and the black-jack leaves shake
In the section between the rivers.
He would slap you on your back and laugh.

Big Billie had a wife, she was dark and little
In the land between the rivers,
And clever with her wheel and clever with her kettle,
But she never said a word and when she sat
By the fire her eyes worked slow and narrow like a cat.
Nobody knew what was in her head.

They had a big boy with fuzz on his chin
So tall he ducked the door when he came in,
A clabber-headed bastard with snot in his nose
And big red wrists hanging out of his clothes
And a whicker when he laughed where his father had a bellow
In the section between the rivers.
They called him Little Billie.
He was their darling.

(It is not hard to see the land, what it was.
Low hills and oak. The fetid bottoms where
The slough uncoiled and in the tangled cane,
Where no sun comes, the muskrat's astute face
Was lifted to the yammering jay; then dropped.
A cabin where the shagbark stood and the
Magnificent tulip-tree; both now are gone.
But the land is there, and as you top a rise,

Beyond you all the landscape steams and simmers
—The hills, now gutted, red, cane-brake and black-jack yet.
The oak leaf steams under the powerful sun.
"Mister, is this the right road to Paducah?"
The red face, seamed and gutted like the hill,
Slow under time, and with the innocent savagery
Of Time, the bleared eyes rolling, answers from
Your dream: "They names it so, but I ain't bin.")

Big Billie was the kind who laughed but could spy
The place for a ferry where folks would come by.
He built an inn and folks bound West
Hitched their horses there to take their rest
And grease the gall and grease the belly
And jaw and spit under the trees
In the section between the rivers.
Big Billie said: "Git down, friend, and take yore ease!"
He would slap you on your back and set you at his table.

(Leaning and slow, you see them move
In massive passion colder than any love:
Their lips move but you do not hear the words,
Nor trodden twig nor fluted irony of birds,
Nor hear the rustle of the heart
That, heave and settle, gasp and start,
Heaves like a fish in the ribs' dark basket borne
West from the great water's depth whence it was torn.

Their names are like the leaves, but are forgot
—The slush and swill of the world's great pot
That foamed at the Appalachian lip, and spilled
Like quicksilver across green baize, the unfulfilled
Disparate glitter, gleam, wild symptom, seed
Flung in the long wind: silent, they proceed
Past meadow, salt-lick, and the lyric swale;
Enter the arbor, shadow of trees, fade, fail.)

Big Billie was sharp at swap and trade
And could smell the nest where the egg was laid.
He could read and cipher and they called him squire,

And he added up his money while he sat by the fire,
And sat in the shade while folks sweated and strove,
For he was the one who fatted and throve
In the section between the rivers.
"Thank you kindly, sir," Big Billie would say
When the man in the black coat paid him at streak of day
And swung to the saddle, was ready to go,
And rode away and didn't know
That he was already as good as dead,
For at midnight the message had been sent ahead:
"Man in black coat, riding bay mare with star."

(There was a beginning but you cannot see it.
There will be an end but you cannot see it.
They will not turn their faces to you though you call,
Who pace a logic merciless as light,
Whose law is their long shadow on the grass,
Sun at the back; who pace, pass,
And passing nod in that glacial delirium
While the tight sky shudders like a drum
And speculation rasps its idiot nails
Across the dry slate where you did the sum.

The answer is in the back of the book but the page is gone.
And Grandma told you to tell the truth but she is dead.
And heedless, their hairy faces fixed
Beyond your call or question now, they move
Under the infatuate weight of their wisdom,
Precious but for the preciousness of their burden,
Sainted and sad and sage as the hairy ass, these who bear
History like bound faggots, with stiff knees;
And breathe the immaculate climate where
The lucent leaf is lifted, lank beard fingered, by no breeze,
Rapt in the fabulous complacency of fresco, vase, or frieze:

And the testicles of the fathers hang down like old lace.)

Little Billie was full of vinegar
And full of sap as a maple tree
And full of tricks as a lop-eared pup,

So one night when the runner didn't show up,
Big Billie called Little and said, "Saddle up,"
And nodded toward the man who was taking his sup
With his belt unlatched and his feet to the fire.
Big Billie said, "Give Amos a try,
Fer this feller takes the South Fork and Amos'll be nigher
Than Baldy or Buster, and Amos is sly
And slick as a varmint, and I don't deny
I lak business with Amos, fer he's one you kin trust
In the section between the rivers,
And it looks lak they's mighty few.
Amos will split up fair and square."

Little Billie had something in his clabber-head
By way of brains, and he reckoned he knew
How to skin a cat or add two and two.
So long before the sky got red
Over the land between the rivers,
He hobbled his horse back in the swamp
And squatted on his hams in the morning dew and damp
And scratched his stomach and grinned to think
How Pap would be proud and Mammy glad
To know what a thriving boy they had.
He always was a good boy to his darling Mammy.

(Think of yourself riding away from the dawn,
Think of yourself and the unnamed ones who had gone
Before, riding, who rode away from *goodbye, goodbye*,
And toward *hello*, toward Time's unwinking eye;
And like the cicada had left, at cross-roads or square,
The old shell of self, thin, ghostly, translucent, light as air;
At dawn riding into the curtain of unwhispering green,
Away from the vigils and voices into the green
World, land of the innocent bough, land of the leaf.
Think of your face green in the submarine light of the leaf.

Or think of yourself crouched at the swamp-edge:
Dawn-silence past last owl-hoot and not yet at day-verge
First bird-stir, titmouse or drowsy warbler not yet.
You touch the grass in the dark and your hand is wet.

Then light: and you wait for the stranger's hoofs on the soft trace,
And under the green leaf's translucence the light bathes your face.

Think of yourself at dawn: Which one are you? What?)

Little Billie heard hoofs on the soft grass,
But squatted and let the rider pass,
For he wouldn't waste good lead and powder
Just to make the slough-fish and swamp-buzzards prouder
In the land between the rivers.
But he saw the feller's face and thanked his luck
It was the one Pap said was fit to pluck.
So he got on his horse and cantered up the trace.
Called, "Hi thar!" and the stranger watched him coming,
And sat his mare with a smile on his face,
Just watching Little Billie and smiling and humming.
Little Billie rode up and the stranger said,
"Why, bless my heart, if it ain't Little Billie!"

"Good mornen," said Billie, and said, "My Pap
Found somethen you left and knowed you'd be missen,
And Pap don't want nuthen not proper his'n."
But the stranger didn't do a thing but smile and listen
Polite as could be to what Billie said.
But he must have had eyes in the side of his head
As they rode along beside the slough
In the land between the rivers,
Or guessed what Billie was out to do,
For when Billie said, "Mister, I've brung it to you,"
And reached his hand for it down in his britches,
The stranger just reached his own hand, too.

"Boom!" Billie's gun said, and the derringer, "Bang!"
"Oh, I'm shot!" Billie howled and grabbed his shoulder.
"Not bad," said the stranger, "for you're born to hang,
But I'll save some rope 'fore you're a minute older
If you don't high-tail to your honest Pap
In the section between the rivers."
Oh, Billie didn't tarry and Billie didn't linger,
For Billie didn't trust the stranger's finger

And didn't admire the stranger's face
And didn't like the climate of the place,
So he turned and high-tailed up the trace,
With blood on his shirt and snot in his nose
And pee in his pants, for he'd wet his clothes,
And the stranger just sits and admires how he goes,
And says, "Why, that boy would do right well back on the Bardstown
                                                            track!"

"You fool!" said his Pap, but his Mammy cried
To see the place where the gore-blood dried
Round the little hole in her darling's hide.
She wiped his nose and patted his head,
But Pappy barred the door and Pappy said,
"Two hundred in gold's in my money belt,
And take the roan and the brand-new saddle
And stop yore blubberen and skeedaddle,
And next time you try and pull a trick
Fer God's sake don't talk but do it quick."

So Little Billie took his leave
And left his Mammy there to grieve
And left his Pappy in Old Kaintuck
And headed West to try his luck,
For it was Roll, Missouri,
It was Roll, roll, Missouri.
And he was gone nigh ten long year
And never sent word to give his Pappy cheer
Nor wet pen in ink for his Mammy dear.
For Little Billie never was much of a hand with a pen-staff.

(There is always another country and always another place.
There is always another name and another face.
And the name and the face are you, and you
The name and the face, and the stream you gaze into
Will show the adoring face, show the lips that lift to you
As you lean with the implacable thirst of self,
As you lean to the image which is yourself,
To set the lip to lip, fix eye on bulging eye,
To drink not of the stream but of your deep identity,

276

But water is water and it flows,
Under the image on the water the water coils and goes
And its own beginning and its end only the water knows.

There are many countries and the rivers in them
—Cumberland, Tennessee, Ohio, Colorado, Pecos, Little Big Horn,
And Roll, Missouri, roll.
But there is only water in them.

And in the new country and in the new place
The eyes of the new friend will reflect the new face
And his mouth will speak to frame
The syllables of the new name
And the name is you and is the agitation of the air
And is the wind and the wind runs and the wind is everywhere.

The name and the face are you.
The name and the face are always new
But they are you,
And new.

For they have been dipped in the healing flood.
For they have been dipped in the redeeming blood.
For they have been dipped in Time.
For Time is always the new place,
And no-place.
For Time is always the new name and the new face,
And no-name and no-face.

For Time is motion
For Time is innocence
For Time is West.)

Oh, who is coming along the trace,
Whistling along in the late sunshine,
With a big black hat above his big red face
And a long black coat that swings so fine?
Oh, who is riding along the trace
Back to the land between the rivers,
With a big black beard growing down to his guts

And silver mountings on his pistol-butts
And a belt as broad as a saddle-girth
And a look in his eyes like he owned the earth?
And meets a man riding up the trace
And squints right sharp and scans his face
And says, "Durn, if it ain't Joe Drew!"
"I reckin it's me," says Joe and gives a spit,
"But whupped if I figger how you knows it,
Fer if I'm Joe, then who air you?"
And the man with the black beard says: "Why, I'm Little Billie!"
And Joe Drew says: "Wal, I'll be whupped."

"Be whupped," Joe said, "and whar you goen?"
"Oh, just visiten back whar I done my growen
In the section between the rivers,
Fer I bin out West and taken my share
And I reckin my luck helt out fer fair,
So I done come home," Little Billie said,
"To see my folks if they ain't dead."
"Ain't dead," Joe answered, and shook his head,
"But that's the best a man kin say,
Fer it looked lak when you went away
You taken West yore Pappy's luck."
Little Billie jingled his pockets and said: "Ain't nuthen wrong with my
                                                                    luck."

And said: "Wal, I'll be gitten on home,
But after yore supper why don't you come
And we'll open a jug and you tell me the news
In the section between the rivers.
But not too early, fer it's my aim
To git me some fun 'fore they know my name,
And tease 'em and fun 'em, fer you never guessed
I was Little Billie what went out West."
And Joe Drew said: "Durn if you always wasn't a hand to git yore fun."

(Over the plain, over mountain and river, drawn,
Wanderer with slit-eyes adjusted to distance,
Drawn out of distance, drawn from the great plateau
Where the sky heeled in the unsagging wind and the cheek burned,

Who stood beneath the white peak that glimmered like a dream,
And spat, and it was morning and it was morning.
You lay among the wild plums and the kildees cried.
You lay in the thicket under the new leaves and the kildees cried,
For you all luck, for all the astuteness of your heart,
And would not stop and would not stop
And the clock ticked all night long in the furnished room
And would not stop
And the *El*-train passed on the quarters with a whish like a terrible broom
And would not stop
And there is always the sound of breathing in the next room
And it will not stop
And the waitress says, "Will that be all, sir, will that be all?"
And will not stop
For nothing is ever all and nothing is ever all,
For all your experience and your expertness of human vices and of valor
At the hour when the ways are darkened.

Though your luck held and the market was always satisfactory,
Though the letter always came and your lovers were always true,
Though you always received the respect due to your position,
Though your hand never failed of its cunning and your glands always
                                    thoroughly knew their business,
Though your conscience was easy and you were assured of your
                                              innocence,
You became gradually aware that something was missing from the picture,
And upon closer inspection exclaimed: "Why, I'm not in it at all!"
Which was perfectly true.

Therefore you tried to remember when you had last had
Whatever it was you had lost,
And you decided to retrace your steps from that point,
But it was a long way back.
It was, nevertheless, absolutely essential to make the effort,
And since you had never been a man to be deterred by difficult
                                              circumstances,
You came back.
For there is no place like home.)
        *

He joked them and teased them and he had his fun
And they never guessed that he was the one
Had been Mammy's darling and Pappy's joy
When he was a great big whickering boy
In the land between the rivers.
He jingled his pockets and took his sop
And patted his belly which was full nigh to pop
And wiped the buttermilk out of his beard
And took his belch and up and reared
Back from the table and cocked his chair
And said: "Old man, ain't you got any fresh drinken water, this here
ain't fresher'n a hoss puddle?"
And the old woman said: "Pappy, take the young gentleman
down to the spring so he kin git it good and fresh?"
The old woman gave the old man a straight look.
She gave him the bucket but it was not empty but it was not water.

The stars are shining and the meadow is bright
But under the trees is dark and night
In the land between the rivers.
The leaves hang down in the dark of the trees,
And there is the spring in the dark of the trees,
And there is the spring as black as ink,
And one star in it caught through a chink
Of the leaves that hang down in the dark of the trees.
The star is there but it does not wink.
Little Billie gets down on his knees
And props his hands in the same old place
To sup the water at his ease;
And the star is gone but there is his face.
"Just help yoreself," Big Billie said;
Then set the hatchet in his head.
They went through his pockets and they buried him in the dark of the
trees.

"I figgered he was a ripe 'un," the old man said.
"Yeah, but you wouldn't done nuthen hadn't bin fer me," the old woman
said.

(The reflection is shadowy and the form not clear,
For the hour is late, and scarcely a glimmer comes here

Under the leaf, the bough, in its innocence dark;
And under your straining face you can scarcely mark
The darkling gleam of your face little less than the water dark.

But perhaps what you lost was lost in the pool long ago
When childlike you lost it and then in your innocence rose to go
After kneeling, as now, with your thirst beneath the leaves:
And years it lies here and dreams in the depth and grieves,
More faithful than mother or father in the light or dark of the leaves.

So, weary of greetings now and the new friend's smile,
Weary in art of the stranger, worn with your wanderer's wile,
Weary of innocence and the husks of Time,
You come, back to the homeland of no-Time,
To ask forgiveness and the patrimony of your crime;

And kneel in the untutored night as to demand
What gift—oh, father, father—from that dissevering hand?)

"And whar's Little Billie?" Joe Drew said.
"Air you crazy," said Big, "and plum outa yore head,
Fer you knows he went West nigh ten long year?"
"Went West," Joe said, "but I seen him here
In the section between the rivers,
Riden up the trace as big as you please
With a long black coat comen down to his knees
And a big black beard comen down to his guts
And silver mountens on his pistol-butts
And he said out West how he done struck
It rich and wuz bringen you back yore luck."
"I shore-God could use some luck," Big Billie said,
But his woman wet her lips and craned her head,
And said: "Come riden with a big black beard, you say?"
And Joe: "Oh, it wuz Billie as big as day."
And the old man's eyes bugged out of a sudden and he croaked like a
           sick bull-frog and said: "Come riden with a long black coat?"

The night is still and the grease-lamp low
And the old man's breath comes wheeze and slow.
Oh, the blue flame sucks on the old rag wick

And the old woman's breath comes sharp and quick,
And there isn't a sound under the roof
But her breath's hiss and his breath's puff,
And there isn't a sound outside the door
As they hearken but cannot hear any more
The creak of saddle or the plop of hoof,
For a long time now Joe Drew's been gone
And left them sitting there alone
In the land between the rivers.
And so they sit and breathe and wait
And breathe while the night gets big and late,
And neither of them gives move or stir.
She won't look at him and he won't look at her.
He doesn't look at her but he says: "Git me the spade."

She grabbled with her hands and he dug with the spade
Where leaves let down the dark and shade
In the land between the rivers.
She grabbled like a dog in the hole they made,
But stopped of a sudden and then she said,
"My hand's on his face."
They light up a pine-knot and lean at the place
Where the man in the black coat slumbers and lies
With trash in his beard and dirt on his face;
And the torch-flame shines in his wide-open eyes.
Down the old man leans with the flickering flame
And moves his lips, says: "Tell me his name."

"Ain't Billie, ain't Billie," the old woman cries,
"Oh, it ain't my Billie, fer he wuz little
And helt to my skirt while I stirred the kittle
And called me Mammy and hugged me tight
And come in the house when it fell night."
But the old man leans down with the flickering flame
And croaks: "But tell me his name."

"Oh, he ain't got none, he just come riden
From some fer place whar he'd bin biden.
Ain't got a name and never had none—

But Billie, my Billie, he had one,
And it was Billie, it was his name."
But the old man croaked: "Tell me his name."
"Oh, he ain't got none and it's all the same,
But Billie had one, and he was little
And offen his chin I would wipe the spittle
And wiped the drool and kissed him thar
And counted his toes and kissed him whar
The little black mark was under his tit,
Shaped lak a clover under his left tit,
With a shape fer luck and I'd kiss it—"

The old man blinks in the pine-knot flare
And his mouth comes open like a fish for air,
Then he says right low, "I had nigh fergot."
"Oh, I kissed him on his little luck-spot
And I kissed and he'd laugh as lak as not—"
The old man said: "Git his shirt open."
The old woman opened the shirt and there was the birthmark under the
                                                                    left tit.

It was shaped for luck.

(The bee knows, and the eel's cold ganglia burn,
And the sad head lifting to the long return,
Through brumal deeps, in the great unsolsticed coil,
Carries its knowledge, navigator without star,
And under the stars, pure in its clamorous toil,
The goose hoots north where the starlit marshes are.
The salmon heaves at the fall, and, wanderer, you
Heave at the great fall of Time, and gorgeous, gleam
In the powerful arc, and anger and outrage like dew,
In your plunge, fling, and plunge to the thunderous stream:
Back to the silence, back to the pool, back
To the high pool, motionless, and the unmurmuring dream.
And you, wanderer, back,
Brother to pinion and the pious fin that cleave
Their innocence of air and the disinfectant flood
And wing and welter and weave
The long compulsion and the circuit hope

Back,
And bear through that limitless and devouring fluidity
The itch and humble promise which is home.

And the father waits for the son.

The hour is late,
The scene familiar even in shadow,
The transaction brief,
And you, wanderer, back,
After the striving and the wind's word,
To kneel
Here in the evening empty of wind or bird,
To kneel in the sacramental silence of evening
At the feet of the old man
Who is evil and ignorant and old,
To kneel
With the little black mark under your heart,
Which is your name,
Which is shaped for luck,
Which is your luck.)

TERROR

"I Volontari Americani Presso Eserciti Stranieri Non Perdono La Cittadinanza."
—Il MESSAGGERO, ROMA, SABATO, 27 GENNAIO, 1940.

Not picnics or pageants or the improbable
Powers of air whose tongues exclaim dominion
And gull the great man to follow his terrible
Star, suffice; not the window-box, or the bird on
The ledge, which means so much to the invalid,
Nor the joy you leaned after, as by the tracks the grass
In the emptiness after the lighted Pullmans fled,
Suffices; nor faces, which, like distraction, pass
Under the street-lamps, teasing to faith or pleasure,
Suffice you, born to no adequate definition of terror.
       *

For yours, like a puppy, is darling and inept,
Though his cold nose brush your hand while you laugh at his clowning;
Or the kitten you sleep with, though once or twice while you slept
It tried to suck your breath, and you dreamed of drowning,
Perjured like Clarence, sluiced from the perilous hatches;
But never of lunar wolf-waste or the arboreal
Malignancy, with the privy breath, which watches
And humps in the dark; but only a dream, after all.
At the worst, you think, with a little twinge of distress,
That contagion may nook in the comforting fur you love to caress.

Though some, unsatisfied and sick, have sought
That immitigable face whose smile is ice,
And fired their hearts like pitch-pine, for they thought
Better flame than the damp worm-tooth of compromise:
So Harry L., my friend, whose whores and gin
Would have dwindled to a slick smile in the drug store
But for the absurd contraption of the plane
Which flung on air the unformulable endeavor
While his heart bled speed to lave the applauded name.
The crash was in an old cornfield—not even flame.

So some, whose passionate emptiness and tidal
Lust swayed toward the debris of Madrid,
And left New York to loll in their fierce idyll
Among the olives, where the snipers hid.
And now the North—to seek that visioned face
And polarize their iron of despair,
Who praise no beauty like the boreal grace
Which greens the dead eye under the rocket's flare.
They fight old friends, for their obsession knows
Only the immaculate itch, not human friends or foes.

They sought a secret which fat Franco's Moor,
Hieratic, white-robed, pitiless, might teach,
Who duped and dying but for pride, therefore
Hugged truth which cause or conscience scarcely reach.
As Jacob all night with the angelic foe,
They wrestled him who did not speak, but died,
And wrestle now, by frozen fen and floe,

New Courier, in fury sanctified;
And seek that face which, greasy, frost-breathed, in furs,
Bends to the bomb-sight over bitter Helsingfors.

Blood splashed on the terrorless intellect creates
Corrosive fizzle like the spattered lime,
And its enseamed stew but satiates
Itself, in that lewd and faceless pantomime.
You know, by radio, how hotly the world repeats,
When the brute crowd roars or the blunt boot-heels resound
In the Piazza or the Wilhelmplatz,
The crime of Onan, spilled upon the ground;
You know, whose dear hope Alexis Carrel kept
Alive in a test tube, where it monstrously grew, and slept.

But it is dead, and you now, guiltless, sink
To rest in lobbies, or pace gardens where
The slow god crumbles and the fountains prink,
Nor heed the criminal king, who paints the air
With discoursed madness and protruding eye—
Nor give the alarm, nor ask tonight where sleeps
That head which hooped the jewel Fidelity,
But like an old melon now, in the dank ditch, seeps;
For you crack nuts, while the conscience-stricken stare
Kisses the terror; for you see an empty chair.

PURSUIT

The hunchback on the corner, with gum and shoelaces,
Has his own wisdom and pleasures, and may not be lured
To divulge them to you, for he has merely endured
Your appeal for his sympathy and your kind purchases;
And wears infirmity but as the general who turns
Apart, in his famous old greatcoat there on the hill
At dusk when the rapture and cannonade are still,

To muse withdrawn from the dead, from his gorgeous subalterns;
Or stares from the thicket of his familiar pain, like a fawn
That meets you a moment, wheels, in imperious innocence is gone.

Go to the clinic. Wait in the outer room
Where like an old possum the snag-nailed hand will hump
On its knee in murderous patience, and the pomp
Of pain swells like the Indies, or a plum.
And there you will stand, as on the Roman hill,
Stunned by each withdrawn gaze and severe shape,
The first barbarian victor stood to gape
At the sacrificial fathers, white-robed, still;
And even the feverish old Jew stares stern with authority
Till you feel like one who has come too late, or improperly clothed, to
a party.

The doctor will take you now. He is burly and clean;
Listening, like lover or worshiper, bends at your heart.
He cannot make out just what it tries to impart,
So smiles; says you simply need a change of scene.
Of scene, of solace: therefore Florida,
Where Ponce de Leon clanked among the lilies,
Where white sails skit on blue and cavort like fillies,
And the shoulder gleams white in the moonlit corridor.
A change of love: if love is a groping Godward, though blind,
No matter what crevice, cranny, chink, bright in dark, the pale tentacle
find.

In Florida consider the flamingo,
Its color passion but its neck a question.
Consider even that girl the other guests shun
On beach, at bar, in bed, for she may know
The secret you are seeking, after all;
Or the child you humbly sit by, excited and curly,
That screams on the shore at the sea's sunlit hurlyburly,
Till the mother calls its name, toward nightfall.
Till you sit alone: in the dire meridians, off Ireland, in fury
Of spume-tooth and dawnless sea-heave, salt rimes the lookout's devout
eye.

*

Till you sit alone—which is the beginning of error—
Behind you the music and lights of the great hotel:
Solution, perhaps, is public, despair personal,
But history held to your breath clouds like a mirror.
There are many states, and towns in them, and faces,
But meanwhile, the little old lady in black, by the wall,
Admires all the dancers, and tells you how just last fall
Her husband died in Ohio, and damp mists her glasses;
She blinks and croaks, like a toad or a Norn, in the horrible light,
And rattles her crutch, which may put forth a small bloom, perhaps white.

ORIGINAL SIN: A SHORT STORY

Nodding, its great head rattling like a gourd,
And locks like seaweed strung on the stinking stone,
The nightmare stumbles past, and you have heard
It fumble your door before it whimpers and is gone:
It acts like the old hound that used to snuffle your door and moan.

You thought you had lost it when you left Omaha,
For it seemed connected then with your grandpa, who
Had a wen on his forehead and sat on the veranda
To finger the precious protuberance, as was his habit to do,
Which glinted in sun like rough garnet or the rich old brain bulging
                                                                through.

But you met it in Harvard Yard as the historic steeple
Was confirming the midnight with its hideous racket,
And you wondered how it had come, for it stood so imbecile,
With empty hands, humble, and surely nothing in pocket:
Riding the rods, perhaps—or Grandpa's will paid the ticket.

You were almost kindly then, in your first homesickness,
As it tortured its stiff face to speak, but scarcely mewed.
Since then you have outlived all your homesickness,

But have met it in many another distempered latitude:
Oh, nothing is lost, ever lost! at last you understood.

It never came in the quantum glare of sun
To shame you before your friends, and had nothing to do
With your public experience or private reformation:
But it thought no bed too narrow—it stood with lips askew
And shook its great head sadly like the abstract Jew.

Never met you in the lyric arsenical meadow
When children call and your heart goes stone in the bosom—
At the orchard anguish never, nor ovoid horror,
Which is furred like a peach or avid like the delicious plum.
It takes no part in your classic prudence or fondled axiom.

Not there when you exclaimed: "Hope is betrayed by
Disastrous glory of sea-capes, sun-torment of whitecaps
—There must be a new innocence for us to be stayed by."
But there it stood, after all the timetables, all the maps,
In the crepuscular clutter of *always, always,* or *perhaps.*

You have moved often and rarely left an address,
And hear of the deaths of friends with a sly pleasure,
A sense of cleansing and hope which blooms from distress;
But it has not died, it comes, its hand childish, unsure,
Clutching the bribe of chocolate or a toy you used to treasure.

It tries the lock. You hear, but simply drowse:
There is nothing remarkable in that sound at the door.
Later you may hear it wander the dark house
Like a mother who rises at night to seek a childhood picture;
Or it goes to the backyard and stands like an old horse cold in the pasture.

CRIME

Envy the mad killer who lies in the ditch and grieves,
Hearing the horns on the highway, and the tires scream.
He tries to remember, and tries, but he cannot seem
To remember what it was he buried under the leaves.

By the steamed lagoon, near the carnivorous orchid,
Pirates hide treasure and mark the place with a skull,
Then lose the map, and roar in pubs with a skinful,
In Devon or Barbados; but remember what they hid.

But what was the treasure he buried? He's too tired to ask it.
An old woman mumbling her gums like incertitude?
The proud stranger who asked the match by the park wood?
Or the child who crossed the park every day with the lunch-basket?

He cannot say, nor formulate the delicious
And smooth convolution of terror, like whipped cream,
Nor the mouth, rounded and white for the lyric scream
Which he never heard, though he still tries, nodding and serious.

His treasure: for years down streets of contempt and trouble,
Hugged under his coat, among sharp elbows and rows
Of eyes hieratic like foetuses in jars.
Or he nursed it unwitting, like a child asleep with a bauble.

Happiness: what the heart wants. That is its fond
Definition, and wants only the peace in God's eye.
Our flame bends in that draft, and that is why
He clutched at the object bright on the bottom of the murky pond.

All he asked was peace. Past despair and past the uncouth
Violation, he snatched at the fleeting hem, though in error;
Nor gestured before the mind's sycophant mirror,
Nor made the refusal and spat from the secret side of his mouth.

Though a tree for you is a tree, and in the long
Dark, no sibilant tumor inside your enormous

Head, though no walls confer in the silent house,
Nor the eyes of pictures protrude, like snail's, each on its prong,

Yet envy him, for what he buried is buried
By the culvert there, till the boy with the air-gun
In spring, at the violet, comes; nor is ever known
To go on any vacations with him, lend money, break bread.

And envy him, for though the seasons stammer
Past pulse in the yellow throat of the field-lark,
Still memory drips, a pipe in the cellar-dark,
And in its hutch and hole, as when the earth gets warmer,

The cold heart heaves like a toad, and lifts its brow
With that bright jewel you have no use for now;
While puzzled yet, despised with the attic junk, the letter
Names over your name, and mourns under the dry rafter.

LETTER FROM A COWARD TO A HERO

What did the day bring?
The sharp fragment,
The shard,
The promise half-meant,
The impaired thing,
At dusk the hard word,
Good action by good will marred—
All
In the trampled stall:

　　I think you deserved better;
　　Therefore I am writing you this letter.

The scenes of childhood were splendid,
And the light that there attended,

But is rescinded:
The cedar,
The lichened rocks,
The thicket where I saw the fox,
And where I swam, the river.
These things are hard
To reconstruct:
The word
Is memory's gelded usufruct.
But piety is simple,
And should be ample.

> *Though late at night we have talked,*
> *I cannot see what ways your feet in childhood walked.*
> *In what purlieus was courage early caulked?*

Guns blaze in autumn and
The quail falls and
Empires collide with a bang
That shakes the pictures where they hang,
And democracy shows signs of dry rot
And Dives has and Lazarus not
And the time is out of joint,
But a good pointer holds the point
And is not gun-shy.
But I
Am gun-shy.

Though young, I do not like loud noise:
The sudden backfire,
The catcall of boys,
Drums beating for
The big war,
Or clocks that tick at night, and will not stop.
If you should lose your compass and map
Or a mouse get in the wall,
For sleep try love or veronal,
Though some prefer, I know, philology.
Does the airman scream in the flaming trajectory?

*

You have been strong in love and hate.
Disaster owns less speed than you have got,
But he will cut across the back lot
To lurk and lie in wait.
Admired of children, gathered for their games,
Disaster, like the dandelion, blooms,
And the delicate film is fanned
To seed the shaven lawn.
Rarely, you've been unmanned;
I have not seen your courage put to pawn.

At the blind hour of unaimed grief,
Of addition and subtraction,
Of compromise,
Of the smoky lecher, the thief,
Of regretted action,
At the hour to close the eyes,
At the hour when lights go out in the houses—
Then wind rouses
The kildees from their sodden ground.
Their commentary is part of the wind's sound.
What is that other sound,
Surf or distant cannonade?

You are what you are without our aid.
No doubt, when corridors are dumb
And the bed is made,
It is your custom to recline,
Clutching between the forefinger and thumb
Honor, for death shy valentine.

HISTORY

Past crag and scarp,
At length way won:
And done
The chert's sharp
Incision,
The track-flint's bite.
Now done, the belly's lack,
Belt tight
—The shrunk sack,
Corn spent, meats foul,
The dry gut-growl.

Now we have known the last,
And can appraise
Pain past.
We came bad ways,
The watercourses
Dry,
No herb for horses.
(We slew them shamefastly,
Dodging their gaze.)
Sleet came some days,
At night no fuel.

And so, thin-wrapt,
We slept:
Forgot the frosty nostril,
Joints rotten and the ulcered knee,
The cold-kibed heel,
The cracked lip.
It was bad country of no tree,
Of abrupt landslip,
The glacier's snore.
Much man can bear.

How blind the passes were!
*

And now
We see, below,
The delicate landscape unfurled,
A world
Of ripeness blent, and green,
The fruited earth,
Fire on the good hearth,
The fireside scene.
(Those people have no name,
Who shall know dearth
And flame.)
It is a land of corn and kine,
Of milk
And wine,
And beds that are as silk:
The gentle thigh,
The unlit night-lamp nigh.
This much was prophesied:
We shall possess,
And abide
—Nothing less.
We may not be denied.
The inhabitant shall flee as the fox.
His foot shall be among the rocks.

In the new land
Our seed shall prosper, and
In those unsifted times
Our sons shall cultivate
Peculiar crimes,
Having not love, nor hate,
Nor memory.
Though some,
Of all most weary,
Most defective of desire,
Shall grope toward time's cold womb;
In dim pools peer
To see, of some grandsire,
The long and toothèd jawbone greening there.
(O Time, for them the aimless bitch

—Purblind, field-worn,
Slack dugs by the dry thorn torn—
Forever quartering the ground in which
The blank and fanged
Rough certainty lies hid.)

Now at our back
The night wind lifts,
Rain in the wind.
Downward the darkness shifts.
It is the hour for attack.
Wind fondles, far below, the leaves of the land,
Freshening the arbor.
Recall our honor,
And descend.
We seek what end?
The slow dynastic ease,
Travail's cease?
Not pleasure, sure:
Alloy of fact?
The act
Alone is pure.
What appetency knows the flood,
What thirst, the sword?
What name
Sustains the core of flame?
We are the blade,
But not the hand
By which the blade is swayed.
Time falls, but has no end.
Descend!

The gentle path suggests our feet;
The bride's surrender will be sweet.
We shall essay
The rugged ritual, but not of anger.
Let us go down before
Our thews are latched in the myth's languor,
Our hearts with fable gray.

END OF SEASON

Leave now the beach, and even that perfect friendship
—Hair frosting, careful teeth—that came, oh! late,
Late, late, almost too late: that thought like a landslip;
Or only the swimmer's shape for which you would wait,
Bemused and pure among the bright umbrellas, while
Blue mountains breathed and the dark boys cried their bird-throated
                                              syllable.

Leave beach, *spiagga, playa, plage,* or *spa,*
Where beginnings are always easy; or leave, even,
The Springs where your grandpa went in Arkansas
To purge the rheumatic guilt of beef and bourbon,
And slept like a child, nor called out with the accustomed nightmare,
But lolled his old hams, stained hands, in that Lethe, as others, others,
                                              before.

For waters wash our guilt and dance in the sun—
And the prophet, hairy and grim in the leonine landscape,
Came down to Jordan; toward moon-set de Leon
Woke while, squat, Time clucked like the darkling ape;
And Dante's *duca,* smiling in the blessèd clime,
With rushes, sea-wet, wiped from that sad brow the infernal grime.

You'll come, you'll come! and with the tongue gone wintry
You'll greet in town the essential face, which now wears
The mask of travel, smudge of history.
Then wordless, each one clasps, and stammering, stares:
You will have to learn a new language to say what is to say,
But it will never be useful in schoolroom, customs, or café.

For purity was wordless, and perfection
But the bridegroom's sleep or the athlete's marble dream,
And the annual sacrament of sea and sun,
Which browns the face and heals the heart, will seem
Silence, expectant to the answer, which is Time:
For all our conversation is index to our common crime.
      *

On the last day swim far out, should the doctor permit
—Crawl, trudgeon, breast—or deep and wide-eyed, dive
Down the glaucous glimmer where no voice can visit.
But the mail lurks in the box at the house where you live:
Summer's wishes, winter's wisdom—you must think
On the true nature of Hope, whose eye is round and does not wink.

RANSOM

Old houses, and new-fangled violence;
Old bottles but new wine, and newly spilled.
Doom has, we know, no shape but the shape of air.
That much for us the red-armed augurs spelled,
Or flights of fowl lost early in the long air.

The mentioned act: barbarous, bloody, extreme,
And fraught with bane. The actors: nameless and
With faces turned (I cannot make them out).
Christ bled, indeed, but after fasting and
Bad diet of the poor; wherefore thin blood came out.

What wars and lecheries! and the old zeal
Yet unfulfilled, unrarefied, unlaced.
At night the old man coughs: thus history
Strikes sum, ere dawn in rosy buskins laced
Delivers cool with dew the recent news-story.

Defeat is possible, and the stars rise.
Our courage needs, perhaps, new definition.
By night, my love, and noon, infirm of will
And young, we may endeavor definition;
Though frail as the claspèd dream beneath the blanket's wool.

TO A FRIEND PARTING

Endure friend-parting yet, old soldier,
Scarred the heart, and wry: the wild plum,
Rock-rent axe-bit, has known with the year bloom,
And tides, the neap and spring, bear faithfully.
Much you have done in honor, though wrathfully.
That, we supposed, was your doom.

O you who by the grove and shore walked
With us, your heart unbraced yet unbetrayed,
Recall: the said, the unsaid, though chaff the said
And backward blown. We saw above the lake
The hawk tower, his wings the light take.
What can be foresaid?

Follow the defiles down. Forget not,
When journey-bated the nag, rusty the steel,
The horny clasp of hands your hands now seal;
And prayers of friends, ere this, kept powder dry.
Rough country of no birds, the tracks sly:
Thus faith has lived, we feel.

EIDOLON

All night, in May, dogs barked in the hollow woods;
Hoarse, from secret huddles of no light,
By moonlit bole, hoarse, the dogs gave tongue.
In May, by moon, no moon, thus: I remember
Of their far clamor the throaty, infatuate timbre.

The boy, all night, lay in the black room,
Tick-straw, all night, harsh to the bare side.
Staring, he heard; the clotted dark swam slow.

299

Far off, by wind, no wind, unappeasable riot
Provoked, resurgent, the bosom's nocturnal disquiet.

What hungers kept the house? under the rooftree
The boy; the man, clod-heavy, hard hand uncurled;
The old man, eyes wide, spittle on his beard.
In dark was crushed the may-apple: plunging, the rangers
Of dark remotelier belled their unhouseled angers.

Dogs quartered the black woods: blood black on
May-apple at dawn, old beech-husk. And trails are lost
By rock, in ferns lost, by pools unlit.
I heard the hunt. Who saw, in darkness, how fled
The white eidolon from the fanged commotion rude?

REVELATION

Because he had spoken harshly to his mother,
The day became astonishingly bright,
The enormity of distance crept to him like a dog now,
And earth's own luminescence seemed to repel the night.

Rent was the roof like loud paper to admit
Sun-sulphurous splendor where had been before
But a submarine glimmer by kindly countenances lit,
As slow, phosphorescent dignities light the ocean floor.

By walls, by walks, chrysanthemum and aster,
All hairy, fat-petaled species, lean, confer,
And his ears, and heart, should burn at that insidious whisper
Which concerns him so, he knows; but he cannot make out the words.

The peacock screamed, and his feathered fury made
Legend shake, all day, while the sky ran pale as milk;

That night, all night, the buck rabbit stamped in the moonlit glade,
And the owl's brain glowed like a coal in the grove's combustible dark.

When Sulla smote and Rome was racked, Augustine
Recalled how Nature, shuddering, tore her gown,
And kind changed kind, and the blunt herbivorous tooth dripped blood;
At Duncan's death, at Dunsinane, chimneys blew down.

But, oh! his mother was kinder than ever Rome,
Dearer than Duncan—no wonder, then, Nature's frame
Thrilled in voluptuous hemispheres far off from his home;
But not in terror: only as the bride, as the bride.

In separateness only does love learn definition,
Though Brahma smiles beneath the dappled shade,
Though tears, that night, wet the pillow where the boy's head was laid,
Dreamless of splendid antipodal agitation;

And though across what tide and tooth Time is,
He was to lean back toward that irredeemable face,
He would think, than Sulla more fortunate, how once he had learned
Something important above love, and about love's grace.

MEXICO IS A FOREIGN COUNTRY: FOUR STUDIES IN NATURALISM

I
BUTTERFLIES OVER THE MAP

Butterflies, over the map of Mexico,
Over jungle and somnolent, sonorous mountains, flitter,
Over the death-gaudy dog whose spangles the sun makes glitter,
And over the red lines which are the highways where you will go.

The highways are scenic, like destiny marked in red,
And the faithful heart inside you purrs like a cat;
While distance drowses and blinks and broods its enormous fiat,
Butterflies dream gyres round the precious flower which is your head.

Their colors are astonishing, and so
Like Brutus, you wrathless rose and, robed in the pure
Idea, smote and fled, while benches burned, from the clamor:
The black limousine was not detected at Laredo.

Tragedy is a dance, as Brutus knew;
But when a little child dies in Jalisco,
They lay the corpse, pink cloth on its face, in the patio,
And bank it with blossoms, yellow, red, and the virgin's blue.

The pink cloth is useful to foil the flies, which are not few.

II
THE WORLD COMES GALLOPING: A TRUE STORY

By the ruined arch, where the bougainvillea bled,
And pigeons simmered and shat in the barbaric vine
And made a noise like Plato in the barbaric vine,
He stood: old.
Old, bare feet on stone, and the serape's rose
Unfolded in the garden of his rags;
Old, and all his history hung from his severe face
As from his frame the dignity of rags.

We could not see his history, we saw
Him.
And he saw us, but could not see we stood
Huddled in our history and stuck out hand for alms.

But he could give us nothing, and asked for nothing,
Whose figure, sharp against the blue lake and violet mountains,
Was under the arch, the vine, the violent blue vulgarity of sky.
He ate a peach and wiped the pulp across his gums;
His mouth was no less ruinous than the arch.

Then at the foot of that long street,
Between the pastel stucco and the feathery pepper trees,
Horse and horseman, sudden as light, and loud,
Appeared,
And up the rise, banging the cobbles like castanets,
Lashed in their fury and fever,
Plunged:
Wall-eyed and wheezing, the lurching hammer-head,
The swaying youth, and flapping from bare heels,
The great wheel-spurs of the Conquistador.
Plunged past us, and were gone:
The crow-bait mount, the fly-bit man.

So the old one, dropping his peach-pit, spat;
Regarding the street's astonishing vacancy, said:
"Viene galopando"—and spat again—"el mundo."

III
SMALL SOLDIERS WITH DRUM IN
LARGE LANDSCAPE

The little soldiers thread the hills.
Remote, the white Sierra nods
Like somnolent ice cream piled up
To tempt a tourist's taste, or God's.

I saw them in the Plaza when
They huddled there like hens, at dawn,
And forming ranks, took time to gouge
Sleep from their eyes, and spit, and yawn.

Their bearing lacked ferocity.
Their eyes were soft, their feet were splayed,
And dirt, no doubt, behind the ears
Did them no credit on parade.

They did not tell me why they march—
To give some cattle-thief a scare
Or make their captain happy or
Simply take the mountain air.

But now two hours off, they move
Across the scene, and to the eye
Give interest, and focus for
The composition's majesty.

The little drum goes rum-tum-tum,
The little hearts go rat-tat-tat,
And I am I, and they are they,
And *this* is *this*, and *that* is *that*,

And the single pine is black upon
The crag; and the buzzard, absolute
In the sun's great gold eye, hangs;
And leaf is leaf, and root is root;
     *

And the wind has neither home nor hope;
And cause is cause, effect, effect;
And all Nature's jocund atoms bounce
In tune to keep the world intact.

And shrouded in the coats and buttons,
The atoms bounce, and under the sky,
Under the mountain's gaze, maintain
The gallant little formulae

Which sweat and march, and marching, go
On errands which I have not guessed,
Though here I stand and watch them go
From dawn to dark, from East to West,

From *what* to *what*, from *if* to *when*,
From ridge to ridge, and cross the wide
Landscape of probability.
They cross the last ridge now, and hide

In valleys where the unprinted dust
Yearns for the foot it does not know;
They march under the same sun,
Appear once more, are gone, but go

Across the high waste of the mind,
Across the distance in the breast,
And climbing hazier heights, proceed
To a bivouac in a farther West.

IV
THE MANGO ON THE MANGO TREE

The mango on the mango tree—
I look at it, it looks at me,
And thus we share our guilt in decent secrecy
   *

(As once in the crowd I met a face
Whose lineaments were my disgrace
And whose own shame my forehead bore from place to place).

The mango is a great gold eye,
Like God's, set in the leafy sky
To harry heart, block blood, freeze feet, if I would fly.

For God has set it there to spy
And make report, and here am I,
A cosmic Hawkshaw to track down its villainy.

Gumshoe, *agent provocateur*,
Stool, informer, whisperer
—Each pours his tale into the Great Schismatic's ear.

For God well works the Roman plan,
Divide and rule, mango and man,
And on hate's axis the great globe grinds in its span.

I do not know the mango's crime
In its far place and different time,
Nor does it know mine committed in a frostier clime.

But what to God's were ours, who pay,
Drop by slow drop, day after day,
Until His monstrous, primal guilt be washed away,

Who till that time must thus atone
In pulp and pit, in flesh and bone,
By our vicarious sacrifice fault not our own?

For, ah, I do not know what word
The mango might hear, or if I've heard
A breath like *pardon, pardon*, when its stiff lips stirred.

If there were a word that it could give,
Or if I could only say *forgive*,
Then we might lift the Babel curse by which we live,
        *

And I could leap and laugh and sing
And it could leap, and everything
Take hands with us and pace the music in a ring,

And sway like the multitudinous wheat
In a blessedness so long in forfeit—
Blest in that blasphemy of love we cannot now repeat.

MONOLOGUE AT MIDNIGHT

Among the pines we ran and called
In joy and innocence, and still
Our voices doubled in the high
Green groining our simplicity.

And we have heard the windward hound
Bell in the frosty vault of dark.
(Then what pursuit?) How soundlessly
The maple shed its pollen in the sun.

Season by season from the skein
Unwound, of earth and of our pleasure;
And always at the side, like guilt,
Our shadows over the grasses moved,

Or moved across the moonlit snow;
And move across the grass or snow.
Or was it guilt? Philosophers
Loll in their disputatious ease.

The match flame sudden in the gloom
Is lensed within each watching eye
Less intricate, less small, than in
One heart the other's image is.

*

The hound, the echo, flame, or shadow—
And which am I and which are you?
And are we Time who flee so fast,
Or stone who stand, and thus endure?

Our mathematic yet has use
For the integers of blessedness:
Listen! the poor deluded cock
Salutes the coldness of no dawn.

BEARDED OAKS

The oaks, how subtle and marine,
Bearded, and all the layered light
Above them swims; and thus the scene,
Recessed, awaits the positive night.

So, waiting, we in the grass now lie
Beneath the languorous tread of light:
The grasses, kelp-like, satisfy
The nameless motions of the air.

Upon the floor of light, and time,
Unmurmuring, of polyp made,
We rest; we are, as light withdraws,
Twin atolls on a shelf of shade.

Ages to our construction went,
Dim architecture, hour by hour:
And violence, forgot now, lent
The present stillness all its power.

The storm of noon above us rolled,
Of light the fury, furious gold,

The long drag troubling us, the depth:
Dark is unrocking, unrippling, still.

Passion and slaughter, ruth, decay
Descend, minutely whispering down,
Silted down swaying streams, to lay
Foundation for our voicelessness.

All our debate is voiceless here,
As all our rage, the rage of stone;
If hope is hopeless, then fearless is fear,
And history is thus undone.

Our feet once wrought the hollow street
With echo when the lamps were dead
At windows, once our headlight glare
Disturbed the doe that, leaping, fled.

I do not love you less that now
The caged heart makes iron stroke,
Or less that all that light once gave
The graduate dark should now revoke.

We live in time so little time
And we learn all so painfully,
That we may spare this hour's term
To practice for eternity.

PICNIC REMEMBERED

That day, so innocent appeared
The leaf, the hill, the sky, to us,
Their structures so harmonious
And pure, that all we had endured

Seemed the quaint disaster of a child,
Now cupboarded, and all the wild
Grief canceled; so with what we feared.

We stood among the painted trees:
The amber light laved them, and us;
Or light then so untremulous,
So steady, that our substances,
Twin flies, were as in amber tamed
With our perfections stilled and framed
To mock Time's marveling after-spies.

Joy, strongest medium, then buoyed
Us when we moved, as swimmers, who,
Relaxed, resign them to the flow
And pause of their unstained flood.
Thus wrapped, sustained, we did not know
How darkness darker staired below;
Or knowing, but half understood.

The bright deception of that day!
When we so readily could gloze
All pages opened to expose
The truth we never would betray;
But darkness on the landscape grew
As in our bosoms darkness, too;
And that was what we took away.

And it abides, and may abide:
Though ebbed from the region happier mapped,
Our hearts, like hollow stones, have trapped
A corner of that brackish tide.
The jaguar breath, the secret wrong,
The curse that curls the sudden tongue,
We know; for fears have fructified.

Or are we dead, that we, unmanned,
Are vacant, and our clearest souls
Are sped where each with each patrols,
In still society, hand in hand,

That scene where we, too, wandered once
Who now inherit a new province,
Love's limbo, this lost under-land?

The *then*, the *now:* each cenotaph
Of the other, and proclaims it dead.
Or is the soul a hawk that, fled
On glimmering wings past vision's path,
Reflects the last gleam to us here
Though sun is sunk and darkness near
—Uncharted Truth's high heliograph?

LOVE'S PARABLE

As kingdoms after civil broil,
Long faction-bit and sore unmanned,
Unlaced, unthewed by lawless toil,
Will welcome to the cheering strand
A prince whose tongue, not understood,
Yet frames a new felicity,
And alien, seals domestic good:
Once, each to each, such aliens, we.

That time, each was the other's sun,
Ecliptic's charter, system's core;
Locked in its span, the wandering one,
Though colder grown, might yet endure
Ages unnumbered, for it fed
On light and heat flung from the source
Of light that lit dark as it fled:
Wonder of dull astronomers.

No wonder then to us it was!
For miracle was daily food—
That darkness fled through darklessness

And endless light the dark pursued:
No wonder then, for we had found
Love's mystery, then still unspent,
That substance long in grossness bound
Might bud into love's accident.

Then miracle was corner-cheap;
And we, like ignorant quarriers,
Ransacked the careless earth to heap
For highways our most precious ores;
Or like the blockhead masons who
Burnt Rome's best grandeur for its lime,
And for their slattern hovels threw
Down monuments of a nobler time.

We did not know what worth we owned,
Or know what ambient atmosphere
We breathed, who daily then postponed
A knowledge that, now bought too dear,
Is but ironic residue:
As gouty pang and tarnished vest
Remind the wastrel bankrupt who,
For gut and back, let substance waste.

That all the world proportionate
And joyful seemed, did but consent
That all unto our garden state
Of innocence was innocent;
And all on easy axle roved
That now, ungeared, perturbed turns,
For joy sought joy then when we loved,
As iron to the magnet yearns.

But we have seen the fungus eyes
Of misery spore in the night,
And marked, of friends, the malices
That stain, like smoke, the day's fond light,
And marked how ripe injustice flows,
How ulcerous, how acid, then

How proud flesh on the sounder grows
Till rot engross the estate of men;

And marked, within, the inward sore
Of self that cankers at the bone,
Contempt of the very love we bore
And hatred of the good once known
—So weakness has become our strength,
And strength, confused, can but reject
Its object, so that we at length,
Itching and slumwise, each other infect.

Are we but mirror to the world?
Or does the world our ruin reflect,
Or is our gazing beauty spoiled
But by the glass' flawed defect?
What fault? What cause? What matter for
The hurled leaf where the wind was brewed,
Or matter for the pest-bit whore
What coin her virtue first beshrewed?

O falling-off! O peace composed
Within my kingdom when your reign
Was fulgent-full! and nought opposed
Your power, that slack is, but again
May sway my sullen elements,
And bend ambition to his place.
That hope: for there are testaments
That men, by prayer, have mastered grace.

LATE SUBTERFUGE

The year dulls toward its eaves-dripping end.
We have kept honor yet, or lost a friend;
Observed at length the inherited defect;

Known error's pang—but then, what man is perfect?
The grackles, yellow-beaked, beak-southward, fly
To the ruined ricelands south, leaving empty our sky.

This year was time for decision to be made.
No time to waste, we said, and so we said:
This year is time. Our grief can be endured,
For we, at least, are men, being inured
To wrath, to the unjust act, if need, to blood;
And we have faith that from evil may bloom good.

Our feet in the sopping woods will make no sound,
The winter's rot begun, the fox in ground,
The snake cold-coiled, secret in cane the weasel.
In pairs we walk, heads bowed to the long drizzle—
With women some, and take their rain-cold kiss;
We say to ourselves we learn some strength from this.

THE GARDEN

On prospect of a fine day in early autumn

How kind, how secret, now the sun
Will bless this garden frost has won,
And touch once more, as once it used,
The furled boughs by cold bemused.
Though summered brilliance had but room
In blossom, now the leaves will bloom
Their time, and take from milder sun
An unreviving benison.

  No marbles whitely gaze among
These paths where gilt the late pear hung:
But branches interlace to frame
The avenue of stately flame
Where yonder, far more bold and pure

314

Than marble, gleams the sycamore,
Of argent torse and cunning shaft
Propped nobler than the sculptor's craft.

The hand that crooked upon the spade
Here plucked the peach, and thirst allayed;
Here lovers paused before the kiss,
Instructed of what ripeness is:
Where all who came might stand to prove
The grace of this imperial grove,
Now jay and cardinal debate,
Like twin usurpers, the ruined state.

But he who sought, not love, but peace
In such rank plot could take no ease:
Now poised between the two alarms
Of summer's lusts and winter's harms,
Only for him these precincts wait
In sacrament that can translate
All things that fed luxurious sense
From appetite to innocence.

THE RETURN: AN ELEGY

The east wind finds the gap bringing rain:
Rain in the pine wind shaking the stiff pine.
Beneath the wind the hollow gorges whine
The pines decline
Slow film of rain creeps down the loam again
Where the blind and nameless bones recline.

they are conceded to the earth's absolute chemistry
they burn like faggots in—of damp and dark—the monstrous bulging
flame.

calcium phosphate lust speculation faith treachery
it walked upright with habitation and a name

    tell me its name

The pines, black, like combers plunge with spray
Lick the wind's unceasing keel
It is not long till day
The boughs like hairy swine in slaughter squeal.
They lurch beneath the thunder's livid heel.
The pines, black, snore *what does the wind say?*

    tell me its name

I have a name: I am not blind.
Eyes, not blind, press to the Pullman pane
Survey the driving dark and silver taunt of rain.
What will I find
What will I find beyond the snoring pine?
O eyes locked blind in death's immaculate design
Shall fix their last distrust in mine

    give me the nickles off your eyes
    from your hands the violets
    let me bless your obsequies
    if you possessed conveniently enough three eyes
    then I could buy a pack of cigarettes

In gorges where the dead fox lies the fern
Will rankest loop the battened frond and fall
Above the bare tushed jaws that turn
Their insolence unto the gracious catafalque and pall.
It will be the season when milkweed blossoms burn.

    the old bitch is dead
    what have I said!
    I have only said what the wind said
    wind shakes a bell the hollow head

By dawn, the wind, the blown rain
Will cease their antique concitation.

It is the hour when old ladies cough and wake,
The chair, the table, take their form again
And earth begins the matinal exhalation

does my mother wake

Pines drip without motion
The hairy boughs no longer shake
Shaggy mist, crookbacked, ascends
Round hairy boughs the mist with shaggy fingers bends.
No wind: no rain:
Why do the steady pines complain?
Complain

  the old fox is dead
  what have I said

Locked in the roaring cubicle
Over the mountains through darkness hurled
I race the daylight's westward cycle
Across the groaning rooftree of the world.
The mist is furled.

 a hundred years they took this road
 the lank hunters then men hard-eyed with hope:
 ox breath whitened the chill air: the goad
 fell: here on the western slope
 the hungry people the lost ones took their abode
 here they took their stand:
 alders bloomed on the road to the new land
 here is the house the broken door the shed
 the old fox is dead

The wheels hum hum
The wheels: I come I come
Whirl out of space through time O wheels
Pursue down backward time the ghostly parallels
Pursue past culvert cut embankment semaphore
Pursue down gleaming hours that are no more.
The pines, black, snore
  *

turn backward turn backward O time in your flight
and make me a child again just for tonight
good lord he's wet the bed come bring a light

What grief has the mind distilled?
The heart is unfulfilled
The hoarse pine stilled
I cannot pluck
Out of this land of pine and rock
Of red bud their season not yet gone
If I could pluck
(In drouth the lizard will blink on the hot limestone)

the old fox is dead
what is said is said
heaven rest the hoary head
what have I said!
... I have only said what the wind said
honor thy father and mother in the days of thy youth
for time uncoils like the cottonmouth

If I could pluck
Out of the dark that whirled
Over the hoarse pine over the rock
Out of the mist that furled
Could I stretch forth like God the hand and gather
For you my mother
If I could pluck
Against the dry essential of tomorrow
To lay upon the breast that gave me suck
Out of the dark the dark and swollen orchid of this sorrow.

KENTUCKY MOUNTAIN FARM

I
REBUKE OF THE ROCKS

Now on you is the hungry equinox,
O little stubborn people of the hill,
The season of the obscene moon whose pull
Disturbs the sod, the rabbit, the lank fox,
Moving the waters, the boar's dull blood,
And the acrid sap of the ironwood.

But breed no tender thing among the rocks.
Rocks are too old under the mad moon,
Renouncing passion by the strength that locks
The eternal agony of fire in stone.

Then quit yourselves as stone and cease
To break the weary stubble-field for seed;
Let not the naked cattle bear increase,
Let barley wither and the bright milkweed.
Instruct the heart, lean men, of a rocky place
That even the little flesh and fevered bone
May keep the sweet sterility of stone.

II
AT THE HOUR OF THE BREAKING OF THE ROCKS

Beyond the wrack and eucharist of snow
The tortured and reluctant rock again

Receives the sunlight and the tarnished rain.
Such is the hour of sundering we know,
Who on the hills have seen stand and pass
Stubbornly the taciturn
Lean men that of all things alone
Were, not as water or the febrile grass,
Figured in kinship to the savage stone.

The hills are weary, the lean men have passed;
The rocks are stricken, and the frost has torn
Away their ridged fundaments at last,
So that the fractured atoms now are borne
Down shifting waters to the tall, profound
Shadow of the absolute deeps,
Wherein the spirit moves and never sleeps
That held the foot among the rocks, that bound
The tired hand upon the stubborn plow,
Knotted the flesh unto the hungry bone,
The redbud to the charred and broken bough,
And strung the bitter tendons of the stone.

III
HISTORY AMONG THE ROCKS

There are many ways to die
Here among the rocks in any weather:
Wind, down the eastern gap, will lie
Level along the snow, beating the cedar,
And lull the drowsy head that it blows over
To startle a cold and crystalline dream forever.

The hound's black paw will print the grass in May,
And sycamores rise down a dark ravine,
Where a creek in flood, sucking the rock and clay,
Will tumble the laurel, the sycamore away.

Think how a body, naked and lean
And white as the splintered sycamore, would go
Tumbling and turning, hushed in the end,
With hair afloat in waters that gently bend
To ocean where the blind tides flow.

Under the shadow of ripe wheat,
By flat limestone, will coil the copperhead,
Fanged as the sunlight, hearing the reaper's feet.
But there are other ways, the lean men said:
In these autumn orchards once young men lay dead—
Gray coats, blue coats. Young men on the mountainside
Clambered, fought. Heels muddied the rocky spring.
Their reason is hard to guess, remembering
Blood on their black mustaches in moonlight.
Their reason is hard to guess and a long time past:
The apple falls, falling in the quiet night.

IV
THE RETURN

Burly and clean, with bark in umber scrolled
About the sunlit bole's own living white,
The sycamore stood, drenched in the autumn light.
The same old tree. Again the timeless gold
Broad leaf released the tendoned bough, and slow,
Uncertain as a casual memory,
Wavered aslant the ripe unmoving air.
Up from the whiter bough, the bluer sky,
That glimmered in the water's depth below,
A richer leaf rose to the other there.
They touched; with the gentle clarity of dream,
Bosom to bosom, burned on the quiet stream.
    *

But, backward heart, you have no voice to call
Your image back, the vagrant image again.
The tree, the leaf falling, the stream, and all
Familiar faithless things would yet remain
Voiceless. And he, who had loved as well as most,
Might have foretold it thus, for well he knew
How, glimmering, a buried world is lost
In the water's riffle or the wind's flaw;
How his own image, perfect and deep
And small within loved eyes, had been forgot,
Her face being turned, or when those eyes were shut
Past light in that fond accident of sleep.

PONDY WOODS

The buzzards over Pondy Woods
Achieve the blue tense altitudes,
Black figments that the woods release,
Obscenity in form and grace,
Drifting high through the pure sunshine
Till the sun in gold decline.

Big Jim Todd was a slick black buck
Laying low in the mud and muck
Of Pondy Woods when the sun went down
In gold, and the buzzards tilted down
A windless vortex to the black-gum trees
To sit along the quiet boughs,
Devout and swollen, at their ease.

By the buzzard roost Big Jim Todd
Listened for hoofs on the corduroy road
Or for the foul and sucking sound
A man's foot makes on the marshy ground.
Past midnight, when the moccasin

Slipped from the log and, trailing in
Its obscured waters, broke
The dark algae, one lean bird spoke.

"Nigger, you went this afternoon
For your Saturday spree at the Blue Goose saloon,
So you've got on your Sunday clothes,
On your big splay feet got patent-leather shoes.
But a buzzard can smell the thing you've done;
The posse will get you—run, nigger, run—
There's a fellow behind you with a big shot-gun.
Nigger, nigger, you'll sweat cold sweat
In your patent-leather shoes and Sunday clothes
When down your track the steeljacket goes
Mean and whimpering over the wheat.

"Nigger, your breed ain't metaphysical."
The buzzard coughed. His words fell
In the darkness, mystic and ambrosial.
"But we maintain our ancient rite,
Eat the gods by day and prophesy by night.
We swing against the sky and wait;
You seize the hour, more passionate
Than strong, and strive with time to die—
With Time, the beaked tribe's astute ally.

"The Jew-boy died. The Syrian vulture swung
Remotely above the cross whereon he hung
From dinner-time to supper-time, and all
The people gathered there watched him until
The lean brown chest no longer stirred,
Then idly watched the slow majestic bird
That in the last sun above the twilit hill
Gleamed for a moment at the height and slid
Down the hot wind and in the darkness hid.
Nigger, regard the circumstance of breath:
Non omnis moriar, the poet saith."

Pedantic, the bird clacked its gray beak,
With a Tennessee accent to the classic phrase;

Jim understood, and was about to speak,
But the buzzard drooped one wing and filmed the eyes.

At dawn unto the Sabbath wheat he came,
That gave to the dew its faithless yellow flame
From kindly loam in recollection of
The fires that in the brutal rock once strove.
To the ripe wheat fields he came at dawn.
Northward the printed smoke stood quiet above
The distant cabins of Squiggtown.
A train's far whistle blew and drifted away
Coldly; lucid and thin the morning lay
Along the farms, and here no sound
Touched the sweet earth miraculously stilled.
Then down the damp and sudden wood there belled
The musical white-throated hound.

In Pondy Woods in the summer's drouth
Lurk fever and the cottonmouth.
And buzzards over Pondy Woods
Achieve the blue tense altitudes,
Drifting high in the pure sunshine
Till the sun in gold decline;
Then golden and hieratic through
The night their eyes burn two by two.

TO A FACE IN A CROWD

Brother, my brother, whither do you pass?
Unto what hill at dawn, unto what glen,
Where among the rocks the faint lascivious grass
Fingers in lust the arrogant bones of men?

Beside what bitter waters will you go
Where the lean gulls of your heart along the shore

Rehearse to the cliffs the rhetoric of their woe?
In dream, perhaps, I have seen your face before.

A certain night has borne both you and me;
We are the children of an ancient band
Broken between the mountains and the sea.
A cromlech marks for you that utmost strand

And you must find the dolorous place they stood.
Of old I know that shore, that dim terrain,
And know how black and turbulent the blood
Will beat through iron chambers of the brain

When at your back the taciturn tall stone,
Which is your fathers' monument and mark,
Repeats the waves' implacable monotone,
Ascends the night and propagates the dark.

Men there have lived who wrestled with the ocean;
I was afraid—the polyp was their shroud.
I was afraid. That shore of your decision
Awaits beyond this street where in the crowd

Your face is blown, an apparition, past.
Renounce the night as I, and we must meet
As weary nomads in this desert at last,
Borne in the lost procession of these feet.

ABOUT THE AUTHOR

ROBERT PENN WARREN was born in Guthrie, Kentucky, in 1905. After graduating summa cum laude from Vanderbilt University (1925), he received a master's degree from the University of California (1927), did graduate work at Yale University (1927–28) and then at Oxford as a Rhodes Scholar (B. Litt., 1930).

Mr. Warren has published many books, including nine novels, eleven volumes of poetry, a volume of short stories, a play, a collection of critical essays, a biography, two historical essays, and two studies of race relations in America. This body of work has been published in a period of forty-four years—a period during which Mr. Warren has also had an active career as a professor of English.

All the King's Men (1946) was awarded the Pulitzer Prize for fiction. *Promises* (1957) won the Pulitzer Prize for poetry, the Edna St. Vincent Millay Prize of the Poetry Society of America, and the National Book Award. In 1944 Mr. Warren occupied the Chair of Poetry of the Library of Congress. In 1959 he was elected to the American Academy of Arts and Letters. In 1967 he received the Bollingen Prize in Poetry for *Selected Poems: New and Old, 1923–1966,* and in 1970 the Van Wyck Brooks Award for the book-length poem *Audubon* and the National Medal for Literature. In 1974 he was chosen by the National Endowment for the Humanities to deliver the third Annual Jefferson Lecture in the Humanities, and in 1975 he was elected to the American Academy of Arts and Sciences, receiving the Emerson-Thoreau Award of that institution. In 1976 he received the Copernicus Award from the Academy of American Poets, in recognition of his career but with special notice of *Or Else: Poem/Poems 1968–1974.*

Mr. Warren lives in Connecticut with his wife, Eleanor Clark (author of *Rome and a Villa, The Oysters of Locmariaquer, and Baldur's Gate*), and their two children, Rosanna and Gabriel.